Humbler Leadership

How to Enhance Your Effectiveness and Enrich Your Life

Josh Wymore, Ph.D.

Published by Leadership Transformation Lab

Fort Wayne, IN

While each story told in this book is true to the best of the author's recollection, some of the names have been changed to protect the confidentiality of the individuals.

For information about special discounts for bulk purchases, contact the author at JoshWymore.com.

Subjects: BUSINESS & ECONOMICS/Leadership | SELF-HELP/Personal Growth | BUSINESS & ECONOMICS/Management

Library of Congress Control Number: 2022922255

ISBN: 979-8-9871025-0-3 (hardback)

ISBN: 979-8-9871025-1-0 (paperback)

ISBN: 979-8-9871025-2-7 (e-book)

Praise for Humbler Leadership

"Josh is a fantastic coach! He has helped members of my team gain amazing insights into their leadership capabilities and make significant progress towards becoming better leaders. The concepts in *Humbler Leadership* will change your thinking about leadership and help anyone who desires to be a better leader."

— Tim Simmons, Chief Product Officer, Sam's Club

"Sustained, differentiated results in business and in life are incredibly difficult to produce. However, *Humbler Leadership* combines compelling insights with practical techniques that literally anyone is capable of implementing. Josh provides an invaluable tool for any leader looking to make an outsized impact in their field."

— Cole Knutson, Principal, Edward Jones

"When empathy eats ego, humble leadership emerges. *Humbler Leadership* gets at the heart of what's missing in leadership today. If you want to truly become a better leader and person, this book is your roadmap."

— Garry Ridge, The Culture Coach and Chairman Emeritus, WD-40 Company

"An insightful articulation of the importance of self-awareness and self-acceptance, authenticity over perfection, ownership over arrogance, and discerning your purpose — with principles and practices for leaders at all levels to develop humbler leadership. I expect great things to come from this book."

— Kelly Schomburg, Senior Director, Walmart

"Humility is foundational for the character of a leader, enabling them to understand themselves accurately and place the mission and organization ahead of their own self-interests. *Humbler Leadership* is a must-read, as it offers a deep dive into how to develop that essential virtue of great leadership."

— Colonel Mark Lessig, U.S. Army, Retired

"If you are looking to invest in your leadership journey, this is the book you need! Practical, compelling, and easy to read. You will love this book!"

"While conducting national searches for C-level executives, humility is a trait we look for when interviewing candidates. Josh's book does a terrific job of illuminating the reasons why."

"Having worked with Josh over the past year, I have personally and professionally benefited from the concepts found in *Humbler Leadership* and believe it to be an invaluable resource for both new and seasoned individuals."

"Josh has done an incredible job highlighting a crucial leadership characteristic that doesn't always get the proper light of day. His take on being a humble leader is sincere and heartfelt; his care for developing humbler leaders comes through his writing on every page. He states that he hopes this book will help make better leaders – I would say, 'Mission accomplished, Dr. Wymore!'"

"We are all 'works in progress,' both on the job and in life in general. This book is filled with great examples of how embracing this mindset can help you become a better leader and a better person."

For Joanna and Jack

Praying you come to embody humility,
and in doing so,
bring shalom to your corner of the world.

Contents

Appreciate Others' Strengths and Contributions

Growth Mindset

Greater Purpose

Introduction

Imagine for a moment that you've been unjustly imprisoned for the last 27 years. After standing up against oppression in your community, you were thrown in jail by powerful people. Meanwhile, they continue to abuse their authority and hurt the people closest to you. How would you feel?

Furious?

Bitter?

Resentful?

Now imagine that your long-awaited vindication arrives. The moral injustice of your situation finally pressures your oppressors to relent, and you are released from jail. Then, in an avalanche of poetic justice, you're also vaulted into the same seat of power that your enemies formerly occupied. Your lifelong oppressors now cower in fear as they wonder what you'll do next. How do you feel now?

Smug?

Delighted?

Justified?

And more importantly, what do you *do*?

This is the question that faced Nelson Mandela in 1994. After years of battling the racist government of South Africa, Mandela was jailed as an insurrectionist. People the world over lobbied for his freedom, but decades ticked by as his prison gates remained locked shut.

And then one day, those doors were thrown open. Mandela was pardoned of his crimes, then became the first democratically elected Black man in the history of his country. Mandela had all the power and moral justification he needed

1

to exact brutal vengeance on his enemies. At the very least, he could punish them fairly for their crimes and ensure that the scales of history would finally be balanced.

What would you do in that situation?

***

What Mandela chose to do still defies explanation for many people. Rather than hauling his former captors into court and punishing them for their crimes, he forgave them. No tit-for-tat, quid pro quo, or "gotcha back." Instead, Mandela pardoned them.

Why would Mandela do such a thing? His decision robs us of the satisfaction we feel when an evil person gets their comeuppance. We feel delight as the evil Emperor Palpatine gets tossed into the abyss at the end of *Return of the Jedi*. We relish watching Hans Gruber flail helplessly as he falls from Nakatomi Tower in *Die Hard*. That's how stories are supposed to end, right? If action movies teach us anything, it's that the punisher will eventually get punished (and apparently fall from a tall building to their death).

Mandela took an unusual approach because he had an unusual goal: to build a unified nation. His purpose was not merely to dethrone Whites so Blacks could claim the seat of power. He wanted to eliminate the hostility between Blacks and Whites and form a stronger country as a result.

Here's an excerpt of the speech he gave at his trial in 1964:

> I have fought against White domination, and I have fought against Black domination. I have cherished the ideal of a democratic and free society in which all persons live together in harmony and with equal opportunities. It is an ideal which I hope to live for and to achieve. But if needs be, it is an ideal for which I am prepared to die.

Mandela's ambitious ideal was not one in which the formerly oppressed could now become oppressors; he wanted to forever eliminate oppression in all forms. He wanted to hand a country to future generations that was better than the one he had inherited. He wanted his country to *heal*. So instead of choosing *retributive* justice, he chose *restorative* justice. He put the country's needs for healing ahead of his own desires for retribution, and in doing so, he embodied the greater purpose that all humble leaders have.

"Nice guys finish last"

We love reading stories about humble leaders like Mandela—people who lead from deep principles and lay down their lives in the pursuit of a greater cause. But let's be honest: most of us aren't lining up to die to our self-centeredness. We admire leaders who live selflessly, but when given the opportunity to embrace humility, we often decline. Why?

Perhaps it's because we implicitly believe the adage "nice guys finish last." Leaders are encouraged to "build their own brands," "raise their visibility," and "sell themselves" to the world, and humility comes across as quaint. Sweet. Outdated. Like the homemade Halloween costume your grandmother made for you as a kid, humility doesn't quite fit you today—and even if it did, you might feel awkward wearing it. In the collision between ideals and self-interest, the ideals get knocked out in the first round.

But what if humility is the missing key to the life you always wanted?

- What if humility didn't cost you the promotion but instead vaulted you into it?
- What if humility enabled you to finally rid your relationships of insecurity, selfishness, and tit-for-tat conflict?

- What if leading humbly didn't cause you to be run over by your peers but instead created more collaboration and buy-in?
- What if humility opened you up to the deeper meaning and purpose you've been longing for?

I'm here to tell you all these things are true. As research shows, embracing humility simultaneously leads to greater purpose *and* performance, stronger teams *and* better results. Whether you're a college intern, an established senior leader, or somewhere in between, humility pays tremendous benefits for your organization and for you personally.

Humility as a second language

Stumbling across humble leadership during my college years changed the trajectory of my life, and I've been a huge advocate for it ever since. I've written this book to share the same vision that inspired me years ago to begin this journey. And after more than a decade of attempting to practice it myself and coaching leaders on how to do the same, my goal is also to help you accelerate your own leadership growth while avoiding unnecessary missteps along the way.

Before moving forward, though, I should make a confession: I'm not a naturally humble person. For years, my pride led me to isolate myself from others, take unwise risks, and offend people I cared about. I still have ankle pain to this day because I arrogantly drove a moped while I had a broken leg. I tanked a relationship with a coworker because I was convinced she was going to fall in love with me. The list unfortunately goes on.

So then why am I qualified to write a book on humility? Shouldn't you be a paragon of a virtue if you're going to write about it?

Maybe it's a laughable premise, but I'd argue my natural *lack* of humility is one factor that equips me to be your guide. For the last 15 years as I've worked to become humbler, I've had to painstakingly figure out every step along the way.

4

Perhaps it's a strange metaphor, but I liken this process to teaching a foreign language you did not grow up speaking. When I started studying Spanish in high school, our teacher wasn't a native speaker. I remember not immediately trusting her capabilities as a result. *We have plenty of native Spanish speakers in Texas; why not hire one of them to teach us?* I wondered.

My perspective changed a bit once I got deeper into the language. As we started to dig into the nuances of verb conjugation, for instance, I realized how many implicit rules shaped the way I spoke English. As we threw endless questions at the instructor about why the sentence was worded a particular way, I wondered how I would handle the same inquiries about my own native language. If a student who was learning English for the first time asked me, "So, why do you say I *am* hungry? Why not I *is* hungry or I *be* hungry?" I would have no clue how to explain the structure of conjugation, let alone irregular verbs. I could explain that most people don't say, "I is hungry," but I couldn't tell you why it's wrong. Because I grew up hearing English from birth, I had internalized all the rules about what to say when. But that pervasive internalization also made it hard to explain the rules to someone else who wasn't steeped in it from an early age.

Here's my point: while a native speaker may be the most natural *practitioner* of their native languages, that does not mean they're also the best *instructor*. Why? Because they can't always relate to the struggles of the nonnative speaker who must fumble through language consciously.[1] And while nonnative speakers may lack some of the nuanced understanding of the language that comes from lifelong immersion, they know how to teach it because they had to learn it—sometimes

---

[1] So you know I'm not making this up, research by Ian Walkinshaw and Duongthi Hoang Oanh substantiates this claim, finding that while native speaking English teachers often pronounce and use the language most naturally, nonnative teachers were best at explaining grammar, crossing cultural barriers, and explaining concepts in the learner's native language.

arduously—themselves. They can appreciate the journey, so they may be better equipped to guide fellow travelers through it as well.

So no, I'm not a native humble person. I haven't always been humble, and depending on the moment, I may still not be. But after years of navigating the process and walking alongside others on this journey, I've discovered some key principles that can help you practice humble leadership more naturally.

---

3 Big Ideas
1. Humility is the foundation of all great leadership **(Part 1)**.
2. Humility emerges as we do, then become **(Part 2)**.
3. Each of us can become humbler than we already are by practicing the mindsets and skillsets of humble leaders **(Part 3)**.

Where we're going

This book is organized around three primary ideas. In Part 1, we'll see that humility is the essential foundation for all good leadership. Rather than replacing your favorite style of leadership, you should view developing humility as a funda-mental virtue that everything else builds on.

Most leaders enjoy working on the flashy parts of their leadership game—building better strategies, making sounder decisions, becoming more effective presenters—but rarely do they devote time to the quiet and slow work of strengthen-ing their underlying character. In workout terms, they love working on their biceps but frequently skip leg day. By embracing the metaphorical squats and lunges needed to become a humbler leader, every other leadership muscle gets a boost as well.

In Part 2, we'll explore the second argument of this book: The best way to truly become a humbler leader is to start behaving and thinking like one today. In other words, what you do shapes who you become. The good news here is that

6

humility is one area of life in which you should "fake it 'til you make it." This is arguably the most contentious thesis of the book, since for many leaders, this sounds like inauthenticity. But that's not what I'm suggesting. Rather, we'll see that changes in our behavior precede changes in our values, desires, and character. If we're serious about becoming humbler, we need to act our way into feeling it. Readers who are itching for practical guidance on their leadership development may want to skip Chapters 3 and 4 and pick up reading there.

Finally, Part 3 shows that we can all become humbler than we already are. Whether you're naturally modest, a born narcissist, or somewhere in between, my goal is not to transform you into a saint but to help you take a few steps farther along the humility continuum. As the title of this book suggests, the goal is to become humbler. Rather than waiting for humility to happen *to* us via a major life challenge or spiritual awakening, I'll show how humbler leadership is something you can intentionally cultivate today.

While many leadership experts have championed the importance of humble leadership (Jim Collins being one notable example we'll discuss in Chapter 2), few have created a step-by-step roadmap for how to become one. This book is meant to pick up where Collins and others have left off by providing that playbook for you.

Whether you're already a believer in humble leadership or you remain a skeptic, I'm grateful you've picked up this book. I hope it challenges your thinking and makes you a better leader. More importantly, I pray it prompts you to ask deeper questions about life and become a better human being. In short, I hope it both enhances your effectiveness *and* enriches your life.

Part 1:

Understanding Humble Leadership

1

Discovering Humility

I've had a few jobs throughout my life I was underqualified for, but none were a bigger stretch than Assistant Softball Coach at LeTourneau University.

Rookie coach

After tutoring a handful of the softball players in precalculus my first semester of college, my curiosity about the team was piqued and I started showing up to practice to catch fly balls. When the team's assistant coach left that summer to take a head coaching job elsewhere, I found myself promoted. As a fan of the sport, I was elated. As a low-income student working my way through college, I needed the money. The only problem was I was absolutely unprepared for the job.

I suspect the coach hired me not because he saw my latent coaching potential but because I was a warm body who would work for a fraction of what he'd have to pay a real professional. In contrast to most of the women I was now coaching, I hadn't started tee-ball at age five. My only relevant experience was playing two half-seasons of high school baseball and coaching a handful of Powder Puff football games. I had plenty of enthusiasm but little competence. In essence, I was the Michael Scott of assistant softball coaches.

I was highly aware of this fact, and I thought long and hard about what to do about it before I stepped into the role my sophomore year. The burning question on my mind going into that first season was: *What do I have to do to be effective?* I'm a reader, so I checked out some softball coaching books from our university's library. I found some old softball VHS tapes there, too. (This was 2005, so YouTube was virtually nonexistent.) I studied everything I could find, but I knew it still wasn't enough. As doubts about my competence loomed large in my mind, I wondered: *How will these players respect a coach who doesn't know what he's doing?*

In my moment of desperation, I came up with a plan. I decided the best way to combat my inexperience was with *confidence*. I knew instinctively that people didn't trust tentative leaders, so I figured boldness would provide the perfect antidote. Like thousands of insecure leaders before me, I determined to make up for my incompetence with confidence.

You might be surprised to learn this approach didn't work as well as I anticipated.

In nearly every practice, a player would question a direction I gave them. Sticking to my untried-and-untrue playbook, I'd unwaveringly declare, "This is the way we're doing it. Get back in line." I was shocked to discover they didn't like that. Somehow, they saw through my thin shell of bravado and detected ignorance slinking in the shadows. However, rather than pitying me and going along with my questionable plans, they resisted—overtly calling me out for my ill-conceived methods or covertly conveying their skepticism through their body language. A few even seemed to detest me for it.

The combination of our ongoing conflict off the field and our terrible performance on it was wearing me out. After enduring a season's worth of infighting and winning a whopping five of our 38 games during my first year, I was exhausted. Our coach apparently felt similarly, as he decided to move on to a less stressful role elsewhere. Consequently, the institution hired a new head coach in the summer of 2006—and that decision would fundamentally alter my approach to leadership.

Jedi mind tricks

I first met Brad Bowser, our new head coach, via a phone call that summer. Within a few minutes of talking to him, I knew right off the bat (pun intended) something was different about him. He seemed much more easygoing than our previous coach, and he was just so *nice*. Normally, that would be an asset, of course. But as I listened to this mellow guy talk about his plans for the team, I thought, *They are going to eat this guy alive.* The movie *Jaws* would be less bloody than what he was about to experience.

I watched Brad with a combination of curiosity and preemptive pity for the first few months. The ladies seemed to be cutting him some slack in those early weeks, waiting to test him out, but I knew the honeymoon wouldn't last for long. Eventually, he would get run over.

One day, I was picking up our equipment after practice when I noticed Brad talking to two of our team's three captains. A few minutes later, I passed the women as they were walking back to their cars. They both had the same dazed look on their faces. I asked them what happened, and one of them said, "Well, we just had a weird conversation with Coach. He said all these really difficult things to us…but he said them in such a nice way it was hard to be mad at him." Brad had challenged them on their attitudes, but because of his kindness, their resistance melted. I laughed at their quasi-predicament and got back to work, thinking nothing of it as they continued their trance-like walk back to the parking lot.

A few weeks later, Brad asked *me* to stay after practice to talk. As we settled onto an aluminum bench in the dusty first-base dugout, Brad began.

"Hey buddy," he said in his gentle and steady voice. "I've noticed you and Stephanie seem to be butting heads a lot recently."

Okay, so this is a confrontation, I thought. *Brace yourself.*

Expressionless, I nodded in agreement. Stephanie was a pitcher on our team, and until recently, a good friend. We'd

13

been cross with each other for the better part of two weeks by that point.

"What's going on there?" he asked, invitingly.

"Yeah, I'm not sure. We just seem to be getting on each other's nerves, I guess." My voice was still emotionless, my defenses waiting to be marshalled.

He nodded thoughtfully. "Yeah, it does seem like that. From what I've seen, you've been pretty hard on her—a lot harder than you are on other players."

I couldn't disagree, so I nodded. He continued.

"What concerns me about this is how it will affect you down the road," he said genuinely. "As a coach and a leader of this team, the tone you set affects the rest of the team. But if this pattern with Stephanie continues, it will really hurt your relationship with her. It will also keep you from growing as a leader."

At this moment, a voice inside my head spoke up. *He's doing the super-nice confrontation thing!* The words he was saying were registering at an intellectual level, but for some reason, all the physical and emotional defenses that normally sprang up in these circumstances were lying dormant. No knots in my stomach; no flush of embarrassment. The hair on the back of my neck remained prone. The absence of anger, judgment, or superiority in his tone meant I didn't have anything to react to. His kindness was like a cloaking shield that was enabling his message to fly under my ego's radar.

"As a man and a leader, you're going to have to deal with lots of difficult people down the road," he continued, without sounding patronizing at all. "And as a leader for this team, I want to see you take responsibility for making this right with her. These are the sorts of challenges you're going to face a lot in life, and this is a chance for you to practice that ability."

Brad continued talking, but I didn't hear much of his message beyond that point. I was lost in thought as my mind raced to analyze how he was doing what he was doing. On the one hand, he was giving me some difficult feedback. At the same time, his delivery of that message was completely anchored in kindness and a desire to see me grow as a leader. His message was tough, but like the players a few weeks before, I couldn't find a way to be mad at him.

In the course of our conversation, Brad basically told me I was being a jerk, that I needed to mature, and that I should start treating this player fairly. But because it was so clear that he cared about me as a person and wanted what was best for me, I felt no defensiveness. In fact, as soon as he finished, *I hugged him.* It was the closest thing to a Jedi mind trick I'd ever seen. I felt more loved during that confrontation with Brad than I felt during even the most pleasant interactions with other people. His combination of boldness and care stirred something in me I couldn't explain. I had to suppress a smile in the middle of the conversation because I was so impressed—and so eager to steal his superpower to use in my own relationships.

As I walked away from the dugout in my own daze, I contemplated what I'd just experienced. What made that conversation with Brad so powerful? How did he do it? Again, it came back to this combination of boldness and love, of grace and truth. Even though he did not yet know me well, his genuine care for me guided all our interactions. Yes, he needed me to get in line for the sake of effective team dynamics. Any wise coach would have addressed my behavior regardless of whether they liked me or not. But delivery was everything. And his delivery communicated a strong, positive regard for me. It told me he was addressing the issue not just because it affected the team but because he knew immaturity like this would limit my success in life if I didn't resolve it. And when someone cares enough about you to tell you difficult things in a loving way, it's hard to get or stay mad for long.

In short, I was in awe of Brad's conversational superpower. I decided, *I've got to figure out how to do that!*

Soon, my passion and curiosity would transform into a deep study of humble leadership—especially after I read a fascinating book about 11 extraordinary companies.

2

Defining Humble Leadership

In the year 2001, the business landscape in the U.S. was turbulent. The adrenaline-fueled economic growth of the late 1990s had just given way to the dotcom bust, and many businesses were reeling in an uncertain world. September 11th added to the confusion, creating further questions about what was stable and predictable. Leaders were looking for answers.

Onto the scenes burst an instant classic of business literature: *Good to Great* by Jim Collins. By analyzing the paths of 11 companies that had vaulted from mediocrity to greatness, Collins and his research team had deduced a handful of timeless business principles that could provide a path forward in a volatile market. The response from the business community was strong, with Collins selling five million copies of the book and reshaping the business lexicon for a generation.

What made the book so captivating was the way Collins captured the differentiators of these companies in such clear and compelling ways. Organizations were clamoring to figure out their "Hedgehog Principle," get their "flywheels" turning, and so on. And the vividness of his concepts was matched by the clear results these companies demonstrated. On average, each of the companies he studied outperformed the market by seven times over at least a 15-year period.

Pause for a second and take that in: *seven times better.* Can you imagine earning seven times more income? Being seven times better at your job? Making your marriage seven times better than it currently is? A sevenfold increase in anything is certainly noteworthy, especially when that increased performance occurs consistently over time.

But beyond the exceptional performance he documented and new business concepts he distilled, the finding that most stood out most to me was the one that also surprised Collins more than any other: how *humble* these great leaders were. During their research, Collins and his team came across a startling trend in each of his 11 good-to-great companies. All of them were led by what he labeled a "Level 5 Leader"— leaders with a paradoxical blend of professional will and personal humility.

Collins described these leaders as a "study in duality." On one hand, they were demanding, fearless, and strong-willed. They raised quality expectations, defeated takeover attempts, cut major lines of business, and challenged family members who were underperforming in their leadership roles. They were intolerant of mediocrity and refused to accept the status quo.

> *Companies led by humble leaders performed seven times better than the competition.*

On the other hand, they were pervasively humble. In contrast to the larger-than-life CEOs who led their competitor companies, these Level 5 leaders were described with words like "quiet, modest, gracious, reserved, understated, and mild-mannered." They didn't seek out the spotlight or hoard the glory. In fact, they were quick to share credit for success with those around them and only turned attention to themselves when it was time to take responsibility for a failure. The driving ambition they demonstrated was always for the company, never for their own careers.

As Collins tells it, he did not expect to arrive at this conclusion. In fact, he purposely tried to ignore it several times. He did not want to write yet another leadership book that gave all the credit for a company's success or placed all the blame for its failure on the senior leaders. But the data were simply irrefutable. Every one of the 11 companies that made the good-to-great leap was led by a CEO with this leadership style, and none of their less-successful peer companies was. The impact of humble leadership could not be ignored.

The impact of humble leadership became clearest when Collins compared the Level 5 leaders to

> *A Level 5 Leader has a paradoxical blend of professional will and personal humility.*

their egotistical peers—leaders like Lee Iacocca, the famed CEO of Chrysler. Iacocca got off to a great start, turning around the failing automaker by slashing expenses, securing new funding, and reducing his salary to $1 as symbol of solidarity. But after taking the company from the brink of demise to an industry leader, Iacocca's success got the best of him. He shifted his attention away from daily operations, instead appearing on dozens of commercials and talk shows. Meanwhile, Chrysler's stock declined sharply.

Rather than handing the reins to a new leader, Iacocca repeatedly postponed his retirement, leading employees to joke that Iacocca stood for "I Am Chairman of Chrysler Corporation Always." He even continued to bleed the ailing company for personal gain after his retirement, reportedly demanding stock options and a private jet. Then, after a mere two years out of the job, Iacocca participated in a failed takeover attempt of his former company. Like a washed-up high school star who can't let go of the glory days, Iacocca seemed compelled to prove himself again and again.

These instances of momentary brilliance were typical for the arrogant leaders who led the *Good to Great* comparison companies. Although these CEOs lacked humility, they still managed to produce results through luck, boldness, marketing savvy, and financial artistry. But inevitably, those results were fleeting. The narcissistic leaders obtained significant wealth, prestige, and power on their path to stardom but left hollow companies upon their departures. Thus, while leaders can attain success without being humble, their stories should always prompt us to ask two questions: "Success by what measure?" and "Success for how long?"

Collins' spotlight on humility soon began to change how the virtue was viewed by business leaders and academics. For many years, humility was seen as a symptom of low self-esteem. However, by the time *Good to Great* arrived on the scene, the new field of positive psychology had been studying humility quietly for a decade. Even still, the concept was not on the radar of the average leader. Most business leaders seemed more focused on mastering this still-new technology called the internet

> *While leaders can attain success without being humble, their stories should always prompt us to ask two questions: "Success by what measure?" and "Success for how long?"*

than they were with developing ancient virtues in themselves. *Good to Great* changed the course of that conversation, swinging the spotlight toward a new (albeit old) leadership trait and accelerating the academic study of positive character traits like humility.

Humility as defined in research

This new interest in humility created a challenge for researchers. How would they define humility or humble leadership? Humility had been lauded as a virtue as far back as Aristotle and remained a core value of many religious traditions, but academics lacked a universal definition that was concrete and measurable.

Drawing from ancient wisdom, classic works of philosophy, and ongoing developments in psychology, researchers began exploring nuanced ways of defining the trait. Some researchers focused on how people thought about themselves; others based their definition on the behaviors that individuals demonstrated. Still others homed in on the impact people had on each other. The result was a varied and divergent understanding of humility. Here are just a few definitions from researchers and thinkers:

1. "Humble leaders admit mistakes and limitations, spotlight followers' strengths and contributions, and model teachability."
2. "Leader humility is a tendency to feel and display a deep regard for others' dignity."
3. "Intrapersonally, humility involves having an accurate view of self—not too high or too low. Interpersonally, humility involves regulation of egotism and cultivation of an other-orientation rather than a selfish pre-occupation with one's own needs."
4. "Humility is seeing myself as *a* person among people rather than *the* person among objects."
5. "Humility is a combination of self-awareness, openness, and an acceptance of something greater than the self (i.e., 'transcendence')."
6. "A leader with the right level of humility is a willing learner, maintains accurate self-awareness, and seeks out others' input and feedback."

So what's the right definition? As is true in most scientific fields, there's no universal agreement. But across the different definitions from research and philosophy, a few components emerge consistently. The most holistic, practical, and measurable definition of humble leadership includes four elements:

1. Accurate self-perception
2. Appreciating others' strengths and contributions
3. Growth mindset
4. Greater purpose

Why these four elements? Let's explore each in turn.

First is an accurate self-perception. A quick review of the prior definitions shows virtually all of them emphasize a high degree of self-awareness (or at least an ardent *desire* to be self-aware, since we'll never be totally objective about ourselves). A heightened awareness of my strengths, weaknesses, and place in the cosmos captures the essence of this theme.

Self-awareness lays the foundation for the components that follow. After all, if I have an inflated view of myself, then I believe I'm self-sufficient, superior to everyone else, and the world revolves around me. This misperception nixes my ability to appreciate others' strengths, adopt a growth mindset, or find a purpose outside myself. Ironically, the same is true if I have a low view of myself. An exaggerated view of my own inadequacy will lead me to be jealous of others' gifts, believe growth is impossible, and focus so much on hiding my flaws from the world that I'll fail to focus on the grander narrative I could be a part of.

> *Humble leadership is seeking an accurate self-perception, appreciating others' strengths and contributions, embracing a growth mindset, and pursuing a greater purpose.*

An accurate self-assessment solves these problems because it properly calibrates my self-image to reality. I realize I have gifts to offer the world, and I can proudly embrace them. I also recognize I am deeply flawed, and I need others who can flex their strengths in areas where I lack them.

Even more transformative is the broader perspective on life that a truly accurate self-assessment brings. If I accurately understand my place in the universe, I recognize I am "*a* person among people rather than *the* person among objects," as *Leadership and Self-Deception* so aptly states. Other people's priorities and values are just as valid (and as limited) as my own. If I fail to make this mental adjustment, it's easy for me to assume that my perspective is the only meaningful one.

However, when I realize the role I play in the universe is small but important, I recognize the world neither revolves around me nor rests on my shoulders. When I take a week off for vacation or turn off my phone on the weekends, I invariably return to an organization that is still functioning without me. When that happens, I understand that while my presence matters, I am not God and the world will keep spinning without my instantaneous reply to an email. By understanding myself in right relation to the universe, I stay grounded.[2]

The second component of humble leadership, appreciating others' strengths and contributions, also shows up in research frequently. While self-aware individuals make good teammates since they don't undervalue or overvalue their abilities, humble leaders go beyond merely working effectively with others and instead draw out the best in their team members.

As the first example definition states, they "spotlight" others' strengths and contributions because they understand the inherent dignity and value of the people around them. Even in the situations where humble leaders possess an unusually high level of intelligence or charisma (or fill in the blank with your preferred leadership trait), they don't ascribe higher value to their own contributions. Instead, they are on a mission to find talent and bring out the best in others. They know they need the gifts and insights of others for their teams to thrive. Rather than waiting for people to offer their gifts, they go hunting for others' unique skillsets.

The third element, growth mindset, is a powerful concept from researcher and educator Carol Dweck that she explores in her book *Mindset*. Dweck's research finds individuals tend to have one of two mindsets about a situation: a *fixed mindset* that believes success in an endeavor is anchored to an individual's talent and that talent is unchanging (i.e., fixed), or a *growth mindset* that believes success is based primarily on an individual's effort and that effort is within one's control. In study after study, Dweck finds growth mindset individuals

---

[2] *Grounded* is one of my favorite terms for humble leaders, for two reasons. For one, my experience suggests that humble leaders are generally the most level-headed and peaceful leaders around. And second, the Latin root for humble literally means "on the ground" or "close to the Earth." Humble leaders understand their place in the universe, remain anchored, and keep their feet firmly on the ground.

outperform their fixed mindset counterparts because they control what they can (their effort) and trust that a sound process will produce superior performance over time.

A growth mindset is essential for humility because it assumes we can all become better through focused effort. Adopting a growth mindset thus requires us to acknowledge our own limitations *and* choose an optimistic outlook for the future.

In contrast, leaders with a fixed mindset may think they've arrived or they're as good as they'll ever be. If that's the case, they have no incentive to learn from others or try a different approach. However, if they come to believe that greater insight or determination can enable them to break through to a new level of performance, they'll be highly motivated to assess their limitations and find ways to improve. When a growth mindset truly pervades a person, it not only enables that individual to grow but also cultivates a hunger for growth itself.

Growth mindset pops up throughout humility research in several ways. Humble leaders admit their mistakes and limitations, are willing to learn from their team, accept feedback on their performance, and avoid coasting on their talents or past performance.

> *Individuals with fixed mindsets resist criticism because it feels like an attack on their innate abilities (and hence, their identity).*

In contrast, individuals with fixed mindsets resist criticism because it feels like an attack on their innate abilities (and hence, their identity). Telling a fixed mindset leader that their presentation was ineffective may communicate to them that they are a poor communicator in general (though the truth may be they didn't prepare well in that instance). Because of their beliefs about the connection between talent and performance, fixed mindset individuals often operate with a goal of ego preservation rather than performance improvement. They perform well to maintain their reputations and avoid looking like frauds or failures.

Growth-minded leaders take the opposite approach, treating feedback as a gift that helps them advance toward their ultimate goal of improvement. Their awareness of their own untapped potential, coupled with an identity that is appropriately detached from their performance in any given instance, enables them to humbly accept criticism. By hearing and incorporating that feedback, growth-conscious leaders improve their processes and enhance their future performance.

These first three components—accurate self-perception, appreciating others' strengths and contributions, and growth mindset—would go far in making us great teammates, partners, and friends. After all, who wouldn't want to work with someone who was self-aware, appreciated you, and was teachable? But these factors alone do not necessarily spark the level of organizational transformation so many companies and nonprofits require today. Effective leaders are also catalysts for change. So what does it take for a humble *person* to become a humble *leader?*

Rick Warren, author of the 35-million-copy-selling book *The Purpose-Driven Life,* identifies the final pillar of humble leadership in the succinct opening line of his book: "It's not about you." Truly humble leaders don't just have an accurate view of their own strengths and weaknesses; they also choose not to focus on their own self-interests. Instead, these leaders connect to a purpose beyond themselves, something grander than their own ambitions. It's this purpose that anchors their decision-making and gives them something to sacrifice for.

In his assessment of Level 5 leaders (what I'm referring to as humble leaders), Collins noted the same theme. Each leader possessed a clear sense of their purpose, and it was never selfish:

> [Humble] leaders are incredibly ambitious. They are fanatic, obsessed, monomaniacal, relentless, exhausting. But their ambition is first and foremost for the cause, for the company, for the purpose, for the work, *not themselves.*

This final component of humble leadership—a greater purpose—completes the definition and distinguishes humble leaders from people who are simply modest. While humble people are open to being challenged, humble leaders are also willing to challenge others for the sake of their larger purpose. Whereas humble team members appreciate the gifts of others, humble leaders recruit strong talent to their teams so their organizations can achieve their compelling visions. And where humble people are *open* to learning, humble leaders *seek out* new knowledge and skills in pursuit of an important goal. These people are "humbitious"—combining humility with ambition.

Frankly, this is where most definitions of humility get it wrong. We assume that the woman sitting quietly in the leadership team meeting is being humble by choosing not to take airtime from her more assertive male colleagues. We believe that the man who fails to champion his team's work is simply too modest to draw attention to his results. But timidity, shyness, and dislike of the spotlight are not humility. It's the greater purpose of humble leaders that prompts them to override their natural aversion to attention or conflict to share their insight or challenge a flawed assumption. They assert themselves not because it benefits them, but because it's necessary to accomplish their greater purpose.

> *While humble people are open to being challenged, humble leaders are also willing to challenge others for the sake of their larger purpose.*

Humility research captures this idea of a greater purpose in several ways, using terms such as "transcendence," "acceptance of something greater than the self," and "keeping one's place in the world in perspective." Across these concepts, one thing remains the same: a rejection of egocentrism in favor of a bigger perspective on the world.

"Learn-it-alls"

So how do all four of these pieces come together to form humble leadership? One exemplar is engineer-turned-CEO Satya Nadella. When Microsoft announced it was looking for its third chief executive in company history, industry experts expected the company to stick with its tried-and-true methodology of hiring leaders who were equal parts razor-sharp and brutally blunt. The company's two prior CEOs, Steve Ballmer and Bill Gates, were both famous for their brilliance and infamous for their intensity. Consequently, many in the industry were surprised when a gracious and modest executive from within Microsoft was chosen to lead the way.

But Nadella was no accidental choice. Having spent the last 22 years at Microsoft, the man knew the company inside and out. He had also consistently delivered results through two traits that stood in sharp contrast to the company's dominant culture: empathy and humility. His life experience taught him these virtues as he and his wife worked to care for a child with disabilities. His eclectic reading of economics, literature, poetry, and computer science also deepened these virtues, leading him to conclude, "From Ancient Greece to modern Silicon Valley, the one thing that has brought down empires or companies or people is hubris."

Nadella's empathy and humility led to some instant culture changes within Microsoft. Senior leadership team meetings soon became collaborative and engaging, with Nadella drawing out opinions of his leaders rather than ripping them apart—a far cry from tense and defensive battles that occurred before. An ardent advocate for the growth mindset, Nadella's stated goal for Microsoft is that they would transform from a bunch of "know-it-alls" to "learn-it-alls"—leaders marked by curiosity, experimentation, and intellectual humility. Rather than using his meetings to show off his own intelligence (which is formidable in its own right), he spotlights the excellent work being produced by the other 156,000 employees in a regular segment called "Researcher of the Amazing." His humble leadership enables him to draw out the best in others and push them to new heights of performance.

One of the most concrete ways this humble leadership is embodied at Microsoft is in its mission and purpose. Gone is the Microsoft-focused goal of "a PC on every desk and in every home, running Microsoft software." Instead, his guiding purpose is "to empower every person and every organization on the planet to achieve more," focusing on the problems his company is solving for the world instead of increasing Microsoft's market share. When asked by a recent college grad why they should consider working for Microsoft instead of one of the other trendy tech companies, his response captured this mentality perfectly:

> If you just want to join a cool company, don't bother. If you want to be joining a company that is going to make *others* cool, join Microsoft. That's what we're all about. We're not trying to be the cool kid or the cool company; our sole purpose is to build technology so that others can create technology. I'll let you choose… what's the more virtuous mission?

Fortunately for Microsoft shareholders, that virtuous mission has not only made the world a better place, but it's also produced fantastic growth as well. When Nadella took the top spot in 2014, Microsoft was expected to continue its gradual decline. *Bloomberg* even ran a story with the ominous headline, "Why You Don't Want to Be Microsoft's CEO." But in his first three and a half years alone, the Nadella-led Microsoft generated more than $250 million in new value, outpacing the combined growth of Uber, Airbnb, Netflix, Spotify, and Snapchat. After seven years at the helm, Nadella's company grew from an impressive $300 billion in market capitalization to a worth of $2.5 *trillion*, making it one of the most valuable companies in the world.

Contrary to popular belief, humble leaders like Nadella don't have to choose between being nice and delivering results.

Instead, they recognize humble leadership as the secret to enabling spectacular performance.

Distinguishing humble leadership from other approaches

But is humility *really* the secret? Students of leadership might look at the stories and definition of humble leadership offered here and skeptically ask, "Isn't this just another name for servant leadership or transformational leadership? What *really* makes humble leadership different?"

Humble leadership is not a competitor to these theories but a foundational element of them. I can't serve others as a servant leader if my purpose is one of narrow self-interest, and I won't invest in people if I don't value their unique strengths and contributions. Humble leadership is a prerequisite, a building block of servant leadership, not a competing theory.

Humble leadership provides this same foundation for other powerful leadership theories like situational leadership or transformational leadership. For a situational leader to adapt their leadership style to meet the needs of their team members, they must first be willing to sacrifice their comfort for the needs of their team. Furthermore, they must have the self-awareness to know what their natural tendencies are so they can effectively compensate for them.

Transformational leaders need humility just as badly. A leader may be able to rely on charisma alone to create a compelling vision. However, to truly inspire others to transcend their own self-interests for the betterment of the team, the leader must be doing the same thing in their own leadership. If the leader fails to embody that greater purpose themselves, cries of hypocrisy will soon undermine their credibility and effectiveness. As with servant leadership and situational leadership, humble leadership is an irreplaceable piece of a complex whole.

To borrow a phrase from my mathematically-minded friend Kevin Butler, great leadership requires "more, but not less" than humility. You need four right angles to make a square, for instance, but that alone is not enough. To complete the shape, must also have four sides of equal length. In the same way, great leadership requires many things depending on your circumstances. You might need to rally a disjointed team through a compelling vision, wade through an ocean of data to identify trends, or lead your people through painful budget reductions. Each of these challenges will require more than humble leadership. But take away humility, and you'll be hard-pressed to be effective. Despite your best efforts to be visionary, insightful, and influential, your leadership will be derailed by self-centeredness, flawed assumptions, and a disengaged team. Humble leadership provides the core strength that every other leadership ability is built on.

Conclusion

As Collins and Nadella both show, humble leadership can create positive results on a large scale. Humility is not just a trait that nonprofit or religious leaders embrace; it can produce serious financial results for the largest companies in the world. And by understanding the four components of humble leadership (accurate self-perception, appreciation of others' contributions, growth mindset, and a greater purpose), we can all move closer to the kind of leadership that Collins describes.

> *To inspire others to transcend their own self-interests for the betterment of the team, leaders must be doing the same thing in their own leadership.*

The seemingly obvious benefits of humble leadership raise several questions for me. Why aren't we all intensely devoted to becoming humbler leaders? Why doesn't every leader have "become humbler" as the primary goal on their leadership development plan? How do we continue to ignore this missing key to our success that's hiding in plain sight?

Perhaps it's because this transformation is easier said than done. Reimagining one's leadership style is a heavy lift, and that large investment should prompt each of us to ask a basic question: *Is it worth it?* If becoming humbler doesn't carry

29

a substantive payoff for you and your organization, then it frankly doesn't merit the sacrifice of your time and energy.

If you're asking this question, you're in luck. As the next two chapters show, humility's return on investment is deep and broad, paying major dividends for humble leaders themselves, their teams, and their organizations. If you're already a believer in humility who needs no further evidence of its importance, feel free to skip ahead to Part 2. But for those of you curious to know what difference humility makes in the world, we'll begin by exploring how becoming humbler makes an individual leader's life better.

> *Why doesn't every leader have "become humbler" as the primary goal on their leadership development plan?*

3

The Personal Benefits of Humble Leadership

Wisdom and faith traditions of all types have been arguing for millennia that humility is important. Reviewing the revered literature of these worldviews quickly reveals most worldviews align on the centrality of this value:

- **Buddhism**: "Whenever I come into anyone's company, may I regard myself less than everyone else, and, from the depths of my heart, value others more highly than I do myself." — Langri Tangpa
- **Christianity**: "I say to everyone among you not to think of himself more highly than he ought to think, but to think with sober judgment, each according to the measure of faith that God has assigned." — St. Paul
- **Confucianism**: "Humility is the solid foundation of all virtues." — Confucius
- **Islam**: "And do not treat people with arrogance, nor walk proudly on earth. God does not love the arrogant showoffs." — Muhammed
- **Stoicism**: "The higher we are placed, the more humbly we should walk." — Cicero

In short, philosophers and theologians the world over agree on this point. As a Christian myself, I too believe you should be humble simply because it's the right thing to do.

regardless of the consequences. It's honestly the most accurate way to understand yourself in relation to the universe.

However, I don't assume that you share my value system or are ready to choose humility at all costs. That's why the arguments I'll make for humility in this book center on a shared value that transcends every religion, culture, and creed: our universal desire to get results.

Although leaders across the globe come from different perspectives, backgrounds, and value systems, one thing we can all agree on is we want to be effective. We want to be good parents, competent professionals, and reliable partners. We have goals we want to accomplish, missions we want to advance, and causes we want to see flourish. As diverse as our individual aims may be, we share a desire to be the best versions of ourselves so we can make our dreams come true.

In my experience, most leaders are interested in new leadership approaches if those tactics can produce better results. The senior executives I coach aren't particularly interested in humility because it is a core tenet of their religions, but they pursue it because it's the most logical and effective way to approach their world and work. Even so, too few leaders understand how valuable humility really is, and even fewer have seen enough exemplars in action to know how to go about practicing it.

The following two chapters are dedicated to those two ends: spelling out the data-driven outcomes of humble leadership and providing some illustrations of how these dynamics play out in real life. In this chapter, we'll review how humility benefits the leaders themselves. In the following chapter, we'll touch on the benefits humble leaders provide to others and their organizations. As this highlight reel of outcomes shows, humble leadership is simply good for everyone involved.

Individual outcome #1: Happiness

A few weeks after my mind-blowing encounter with Brad's Jedi mind tricks, I got my first opportunity to try and replicate his success. On a breezy spring afternoon, I was running a drill for our outfielders when one of the players stormed over to explain why I was doing it the wrong way. This mid-drill confrontation coming my way was one I was intimately familiar with, having done this same dance a dozen times with this particular player.

I unfortunately knew exactly how the script would play out. She'd ask a question or make a suggestion—sometimes graciously, sometimes demandingly—and regardless, I'd shut it down to maintain my semblance of authority. Then she'd get mad, and we'd argue in front of the other players until she stormed to the back of the line to finish the drill.

Whether she was right or not was never a factor in the equation. Because I was insecure, I couldn't tolerate a challenge to my authority even if I was dead wrong. I had to appear to be in control, and listening to *a player* when I was the coach was the opposite of being in control. In those moments, I never had any intentions of listening or adapting—just explaining and defending. My identity as a knowledgeable coach was being threatened in those moments, and when that happened, I responded defensively and tried not to look weak.

But this time as she stormed over to me, my mind started racing, trying to figure out a way to use the superpower I had stolen from Brad to write a different ending to this story. Sure enough, she approached and started critiquing my setup of the drill. I listened to her patiently instead of interrupting (big win already), and when she finished, I said, "You know what? You're making a lot of good points. I do think there are probably some better ways to design the drill. I don't want to stop practice right now to sort through all those options, but if you don't mind hanging around after we're done, we can talk through the drill and brainstorm the best way to do it."

Her response was total shock. Her mouth hung open for a full three seconds. In all the time I'd been her coach, she'd never heard me come close to admitting I was wrong, and I'd never once asked for help. So after what felt like an eternity, she agreed in a sort of dazed way—a look that reminded me a lot of the one I had seen on the captains' faces a few weeks prior—and trotted back to the line.

I was elated. Not only did the conversation go shockingly well, but for the first time in my life, I realized *I didn't have to be right every time to be a good leader.* While this is an obvious realization, very few of us live like this is true. We do verbal gymnastics to avoid saying we were wrong. (My favorite is, "Mistakes were made" rather than "I made a mistake.") We explain in condescending tones to others how while it might seem like we're wrong, they're actually the one who is mistaken. And we dodge difficult questions because we'd rather look smart than get to the bottom of an issue.

In that moment, I felt something I hadn't felt as a softball coach before: peace. Having dropped the façade of invulnerability and survived, I could breathe easier—exhaling some of the stress that had been building in me like the swelling on an overworked knee. For once, I had hope things might be different. Maybe, just maybe, I could afford to get off the hamster wheel of trying to prove I was smart enough or good enough and be a human being. Maybe I could actually enjoy being a coach.

***

It turns out I'm not alone in experiencing greater joy, peace, and security because of humility. In a national survey of 3,010 individuals, University of Michigan professor Neal Krause and his colleagues explored the connection between humility, stressful life events, anxiety, depression, and happiness. Their core question was, "Does humility make a difference in people's quality of life after they've encountered stressful events such as a serious illness, family troubles, or death of a close friend?"

What they found was significant. Individuals who scored higher on a humility assessment experienced:

- 57% fewer depressive symptoms
- 64% less anxiety
- 73% more happiness
- 56% greater life satisfaction

Interestingly, the effects were the strongest when stress was at its highest. While humble people were happier with their lives in general, humility had an even greater effect on depression, anxiety, happiness, and satisfaction when individuals had experienced several stressful life events. Humility not only improves the quality of your day-to-day life, it also protects your psychological well-being during stressful seasons.

Likewise, one pillar of humble leadership, growth mindset, shows similar effects on mental wellness. One meta-analysis of 72 studies on growth mindset found a meaningful correlation between the mindset and psychological distress. Individuals who believed their success was not limited by their talent but could instead be increased through thoughtful effort were less despondent when difficult life circumstances arose. They maintained a sense of control over their future, so they could channel their energy into a productive path forward.

> *Humility not only improves the quality of your day-to-day life, it also protects your psychological well-being during stressful seasons.*

Because of our culture of hero worship, most of us have come to believe good leaders are the people who don't have problems. We then pretend to be someone who has it all together so people think we're good leaders. But the truth is, none of us have it all together. Most of us don't even have half of "it" together. But we desperately fight to maintain the mirage, if only for ourselves. So we defend ourselves, deflect blame, and try to move on as quickly as we can. It's exhausting, and the sad fact is, the only folks we're fooling are ourselves.

Those around us see through the smoke and mirrors and respect us less. As leadership expert Craig Groeschel artfully says, "People would rather follow a leader who is always *real* rather than one who is always *right*." We think others are looking for a perfect leader when what they want most is an authentic one.

Humility offers a path out of this trap. Since humble leaders can separate their identity from their performance, they gain greater stability during life's uncertain circumstances. Their grounded perspective about their place in the universe creates greater objectivity, enabling them to effectively navigate difficult circumstances and emerge whole. And when they fail (as we all do), they focus on improving what they can control rather than flailing to micromanage things outside their domain. As a result, humble leaders are more grounded, stable, and happy than the rest of us.

> *Humble leaders can separate their identity from their performance.*

Individual outcome #2: Stronger relationships

It's no exaggeration to say that Pete Carroll is one of the most successful coaches in football history. Before winning the 2012 Super Bowl with the Seattle Seahawks, Carroll won back-to-back national championships with the University of Southern California Trojans (USC), making him one of only three coaches who've won both professional and collegiate football championships. But what makes Carroll stand out even more than his win-loss record is his philosophy as a coach.

Carroll first clarified his coaching philosophy while taking a one-year hiatus from football after getting fired from the New England Patriots in 1997. This first attempt at a coherent coaching system placed competition, excellence, and learning from mistakes at the core. He would embody these principles through practices like "Tell the Truth Monday" where players and coaches would study game film to accurately assess where they succeeded, where they failed, and how they could get better. Everything would be focused on improving from one day to the next.

Carroll first implemented his "always compete" philosophy as the head coach at USC. His coaching strategy soon bore fruit—helping him lead his team to an 11–2 record in just his second season—but he kept refining it all the same. Competition continued to take center stage in his priorities, but he soon began to define the term more holistically, returning to its Latin roots where it was defined as "striving together" (*com*, meaning, "with or together," and *petere*, meaning, "aim at or seek"). Carroll came to realize that when players pushed themselves to improve their past performance, the focus on self-improvement was contagious. The drive for individual excellence soon turned into a focus on team excellence, elevating everyone's performance along the way.

But as Carroll continued to hone his core beliefs, he realized that a value even more important than competition undergirded everything he did. That value was *caring*. He describes it this way:

> I didn't always know this, but now I realize that it's the caring for others that is the real key to success. It's driven us to consistently seek an appreciation for the unique and special qualities of each individual. It's this caring that creates the bond that allows teams to do great things together. I've learned when this relationship develops, we're really hard to beat...and to me, that's what competing is all about.

In his drive to be the best, Carroll discovered that caring for his coaches and players took his team's performance to an even higher level. Rather than trying to squeeze the *most* out of people, he started focusing on bringing out their *best*. He goes on:

> The essence of this is simply about caring for other people. If you care about people, you elevate their own

self-worth. You coach up their strengths, and that makes them more powerful than they already are.

This isn't a New-Age deal. This isn't rocket science. This is just humanness. I think this is tapping into what's really extraordinarily valuable and important in being human.

While Carroll's focus on competition certainly resonated within the athletic community, his emerging emphasis on caring raised eyebrows among many football traditionalists. In a world that idolized the command-and-control model of football coaching, Carroll's approach felt vulnerable. Touchy-feely. "Left Coast."

But skeptics of Carroll's positivity and focus on relationships were soon won over by the results. His deep interest in the backgrounds and motivations of his players made him a superb recruiter at the collegiate level, enabling him to sign 53 future NFL draft picks to his USC teams. After he left the Trojans for the Seattle Seahawks, his attention to the uniqueness of others enabled him to spot talent hidden deep in the draft. Whenever he signed new players, his drive to help them discover their own philosophy and purpose enabled him to connect with them on a much deeper level than many other coaches and players could.

The result was that the team deeply bought into his approach and performed better, too. As Seattle quarterback Russell Wilson notes, "You can tell he really cares about his players...That's what's special." Former assistant coach Dan Quinn also felt the impact:

With other coaches, I wanted to do my job really well for myself. With Pete, I wanted to do a really good job for him. I wanted to deliver for him. I didn't want to let him down.

Carroll's caring-first philosophy created stronger relationships between him and his players. As one sportswriter summed it up, "It's not about winning on Sunday, or about winning a Super Bowl. It's about creating the type of atmosphere that drives athletes to want to win every day, together." By focusing less on the win-loss record and more on his greater purpose of caring for others, Carroll found that players worked harder for him.

But the coach's impact did not just end with how they felt about him. It also seeped into the culture of the team in general. Seahawks star Doug Baldwin described the dynamic this way:

> There's this thing on the football field when you do something, like block or break a tackle. You can do it because you know that if you do it well, it will add to your stats and you can make more money. But when you have an emotional connection to the guy next to you, you're going to fight even harder for him. So when Marshawn [Lynch] is running down the sideline, you see guys sprinting their hearts out to go block for him because they love him, they care for him. That was the kind of culture we built there and it was pretty powerful to be a part of.

***

When I began researching Carroll's story, I assumed the headline would be "Humble leadership drives better team performance." After all, Carroll demonstrates aspects of all four of the humble leadership components: fostering an accurate self-perception by learning from his past performance, leveraging the strengths of others by drawing out their potential, embracing a growth mindset by focusing on performing in the moment rather than fixating on the outcome, and cultivating a grander purpose by investing into relationships as an end in themselves

However, the more I learned about Carroll, the more I saw a different headline emerging: "Humble leadership fosters deep relationships." Of all the notable outcomes he achieved, the most compelling aspect of his story for me was the genuine personal relationships he forged amongst football players. These hulking men play a notoriously violent sport in an industry with a reputation for being highly transactional and egocentric. Yet somehow Carroll's caring slices through all this noise in Ted Lasso fashion to foster genuine connections with his players and coaches. His deep appreciation for others' strengths—the aspect of humble leadership that shines brightest for him—is the catalyst for relationships that will likely last even longer than the glow of a Super Bowl win.

It turns out that the kind of deep relationships that Carroll experienced are quite common for humble people. A survey of 1,500 people by University of Arkansas professor H. Wallace Goddard and his colleagues found that wives were more satisfied with their marriages when their husbands displayed humble traits. In fact, humility proved to be a better predictor of marital satisfaction than how compassionate their spouse was or how objectively stressful their marriage was.

Several factors can explain this result. Humble individuals are more empathetic, enabling them to forge stronger bonds with their spouses. When combined with the fact that a humble mindset naturally leads people to become more helpful, for-giving, generous, grateful, and cooperative, it's no surprise that humble spouses are more fun to be around.

I can testify to the validity of this outcome personally. Few things are more humbling for me than when my wife and I are having an argument (what she calls a "disagreement"), and instead of her lobbing the blame grenade back over to my side, she steps back, apologizes for her contributions to the problem, and asks for forgiveness. Ironically, it does not prompt the "I told you so" victory dance we often fear, but instead leads me to lower my guard and look for ways I was wrong, too. In these ways, apologizing promotes self-awareness for both the apologizer and the recipient.

Humble leaders know this secret intuitively. By seeking to understand their own faults and take ownership of them, they control what they can control—and find others tend to reciprocate. By appreciating the strengths and contributions of others, they reduce the competitive drive to be right that often prevents relationships from overcoming conflict. As they embrace a growth mindset, they recognize they are intrinsically flawed and seek to learn from those mistakes rather than cover them up. And by making their greater purpose a healthy relationship rather than one that is merely absent of conflict, they are willing to confront the thorny problems that hinder true harmony. Humility alone is not a foolproof plan for a happy relationship, but it's certainly hard to have a great one without it.

> *Apologizing promotes self-awareness for both the apologizer and the recipient.*

Individual outcome #3: Performance

During my first year of college, I met a nontraditional student named Greg. Greg was easy to spot in a class of 17- and 18-year-olds, as he was the only one of us who was balding and rocking a sweet salt-and-pepper mustache. In our class of scraggly first-years, he looked more like a retired firefighter than a stereotypical precalculus student.

After delaying college for years while he worked and raised a family, Greg finally decided it was time to complete what he'd left undone and go back to get his bachelor's degree. Despite having a full-time job and a couple of kids at home, he managed to squeeze a full slate of classes into his already-busy life. And like most other nontraditional students, he also had to re-learn how to learn in an academic setting. As a tradesman and father, he had plenty of life experience to offer, but his precalculus skills had accumulated 20 years of rust. It was that rust that prompted our paths to intersect.

To help pay for college, I'd signed up to be a math tutor. The job was great, as it allowed me to earn a good hourly rate, help other people, and explore what a future in education might be like. But I wasn't anticipating the challenge of tutoring someone who was almost my dad's age. At a meager 17 years old, I felt insecure when Greg signed up for a session with me. I half expected him to ask for a different tutor once he realized I was just a few years older than his own teenager.

But Greg couldn't have been a better pupil. He was determined to learn and get better. He'd bring his half-solved problems to our tutoring sessions and soak up everything we talked about. This guy was working a full-time job, caring for a family, and driving over to a college campus at night to learn from a teenager. He was hungry.

Greg was also the dream group project member. He worked hard, asked good questions, and learned from everyone around him. He graduated on time and with good grades despite all the other life circumstances he faced. His combination of humility and purpose drove him to succeed—and humbled me in the process. With all the free time and natural math aptitude I had, I didn't have to be as focused and determined as he did. His example stuck with me, spurring me on to be the best I could be.

***

As I would later learn from research, humble people like Greg experience these sorts of performance boosts all the time. Research by Brad Owens, Michael Johnson, and Terrence Mitchell found that humbler students outperformed their less humble peers. In group projects, humble students were more likely to draw on the strengths of others rather than trying (and failing) to do it all on their own. Because they possessed an accurate self-perception, they knew their limits and where others could add value. They consequently avoided overextending themselves, instead bringing the best out of others around them. Arrogant individuals, in contrast, overestimated their abilities and failed to prepare adequately for challenging tasks. They felt unwarranted confidence in their own abilities, leading them to do more poorly overall.

Not only did humble individuals perform better on individual tasks throughout the year, but their team members rated their contributions to the group more highly as well. In a finding that surprised no one who has ever participated in a group project, the team members who were more appreciative of their teammates were more fun to work with and enabled the group to get more done.

But the most surprising twist of the study was how humility and intelligence intersected in their research. Shockingly, humble people with low IQs *outperformed* smart people who lacked humility. Teachability, not raw ability, made the greatest difference in long-term performance.

How does humility make you smarter? As Owens and his colleagues summarized in their findings, humility enables people to use their raw abilities more effectively. It's humility, not high SAT scores, that enables someone to accurately assess where they need to improve and devote the right amount of effort to grow in that area. Humble leaders can leverage their own abilities (even if they're limited) far more effectively than their more talented but less self-aware peers can. As a result, they improve faster and perform better in academic settings.

> *Humble people with low IQs actually outperformed smart people who lacked humility.*

My friend Greg nailed his precalculus class not because he was a high school valedictorian or because he scored perfectly on his SAT. He delivered results because he had the humility to recognize where he needed help and draw on the skills of someone else to shore up those weaknesses.

This performance boost doesn't just apply to academics; it translates to the workplace, too. Researchers at Baylor University found individuals who were both honest and humble consistently received higher performance reviews than their peers. Similarly, research by Owens and Hekman finds that humble people are better at identifying and cultivating opportunities because they're less consumed with avoiding mistakes. Because they are more secure personally, more open to learning from failure, and less likely to base their identities on maintaining an aura of perfection, they are freer to take smart risks and pursue opportunities—a distinction that researchers call a "promotion focus" (looking to promote good outcomes) versus a "prevention focus" (looking to prevent poor outcomes).

> *Teachability, not raw ability, made the greatest difference in long-term performance.*

But one above-and-beyond performance enhancer for humble leaders may be the clearer sense of purpose they possess. During my previous stint in higher education, I worked closely with many adult students like Greg who were going back to school. Some adopted a transactional focus, just looking to obtain their degrees as quickly as possible so they could be eligible for a promotion at work. But most of them had far bigger reasons for returning to school. They wanted to keep a promise to a loved one, be the first person in their family to cross the graduation stage, or inspire their children to push themselves further.

As research shows, having a compelling purpose that's larger than yourself consistently drives this kind of increased performance. To test the power of purpose for performance, Wharton professor and psychologist Adam Grant and his research team designed an experiment for college students who were paid to raise money by calling potential donors.

After splitting up the students randomly into three test groups, the researchers gave different stimuli to each set. While the first group of students experienced no change in their daily routine, the second group took five minutes to read a letter from a student who had benefited from the money that these students were raising. The third group read the letter and spent five minutes with the student to ask questions and make a personal connection. A month after this brief experience,

Grant and his team returned and asked, "Did either of these interventions make a difference?"

The answer was an unequivocal *yes*. While reading the letter seemed to have no effect on the performance of the second group, students who met their beneficiary showed more perseverance in staying on the phone longer (a tough task for anyone who's ever worked a phonathon) and raised more money. And not just a little more—a *lot* more. The third group who formed a personal connection with their beneficiary spent 142% more time on the phone and raised 171% more money than those who had read nothing and met no one. That brief connection with their greater purpose—only lasting five minutes—still carried an impact on these students' lives a month after the fact.

If you're a natural skeptic, you could argue this boost in performance just comes down to additional motivation. Sure, these callers performed better, but they probably would have done just as well if given a bonus or some other kind of motivation. Is it essential for their purpose to connect to something outside of themselves?

In a second experiment with motivating student fundraisers, Grant addressed this question directly. As in his first study, he created three groups: a control group who received no stimuli, a group who read a letter about how their work benefited scholarship students, and a third who read letters from former callers who attested to how this job experience had helped them advance their own careers. In other words, one treatment group was reminded of how their work benefited others, while the other was reminded of how their work benefited themselves.

> *Purpose-driven fundraisers raised 171% more money than their peers.*

Again, the power of a larger purpose shone through. As in the previous experiment, students who were reminded of their impact on others more than doubled the money they raised a month later. And the students who were focused on themselves? No improvement. Focusing on themselves did not deliver the same degree of motivation, perseverance, and performance that a commitment to a larger purpose did.

Herein lies the promise for humble people. As purpose-driven people, their grander mission can motivate them to overcome obstacles, stay focused amidst distractions, and sacrifice for the greater good. Regardless of whether they are serving in a prominent leadership role or on the front lines of their organizations, their purpose compels them to persevere toward their goals.

Conclusion

If you're an ambitious leader, you undoubtedly have a mental list of things you want to want to improve at. But regardless of what tops your list, you'd be hard pressed to find a character trait that pays greater dividends for you personally than humility. If you want to live a happier, less stressful life, humility provides the foundation. Want to strengthen your relationships with your boss, peers, or family? Humility must come first. And if you're looking to separate yourself from the pack with stronger individual performance, humility gives you the tools to do just that. Becoming humbler will just make your life better, period.

But even if that fact weren't true, those of us in leadership positions would have a professional obligation to focus on humility simply because of the impact it has on those we lead. As the next chapter shows, while humility pays significant dividends for individual performers, some of its greatest outcomes are for the people and the organizations that humble leaders serve.

4

Humble Leadership's ROI

As we explored in the previous chapter, humility drives several important benefits for us personally. This evidence alone could provide all the motivation we need to cultivate this character trait. After all, who wouldn't want to be happier, better connected to others, and performing at their peak?

But for leaders who need more incentives beyond self-improvement, the good news is that becoming humbler does not benefit us alone. The return on investment for our organizations is huge. As research shows, humble leadership drives greater employee engagement, healthier organizational cultures, and stronger bottom-line results.

Organizational outcome #1: Engagement

One of the humblest executives I've had a chance to observe up close is Dr. Kim Hayworth. Kim and I worked together at the same small private university for four years and had many opportunities to collaborate—she as the Vice President for Student Success and I as the Executive Director of our adult and graduate studies operations. During that time, I was consistently impressed by her humble leadership.

As one of her colleagues, I had multiple opportunities to see her steer meetings and shape conversations while the pressure was on. In every interaction I observed, I was struck by how she always seemed to have three goals: serving students, partnering with others, and advancing the university. Higher education is notorious for its fiefdoms and political battles, yet Kim refused to fight turf wars to protect her budget or headcount. She always brought the conversation back to the mission, not her legacy or pet project. Even when her responsibilities required her to take policy positions that were unpopular with students, she remained gracious, teachable, and invested in dialogue.

For me, though, Kim's greatest credibility came not from what I observed directly but from what my wife had to say about her. As one of Hayworth's team members, Emily regularly witnessed her leadership in action and frequently reflected on Kim's self-awareness, other-centeredness, and care for her team. Seeing my wife flourish under her humble leadership multiplied my esteem for Kim even further.

It's hard to put someone's humility into words when you know them well, especially because the virtue is often defined by the absence of behavior (i.e., not being self-promoting). I knew that Kim's department was remarkably drama-free, and I attributed much of the team's health to her steady hand at the helm. But to ensure I wasn't biased in my view—and to collect some additional words for what I felt intuitively—I interviewed two of her former direct reports to get their take on their boss. Both emphatically agreed with my assessment but also struggled to put their finger on exactly what it was that made her different.

For Dan, an Associate Vice President who reported to Kim for 15 years, it was the thousand small things Kim did. The way she worked long hours but never played the martyr card. How she looked for opportunities to catch people doing the right things so she could thank them. The fact that she mentored individual students for free and stayed connected with them after graduation. As Dan describes, she was even positive when pushing him to grow:

> When she suggested professional development opportunities for me, she'd say, "You're a great leader—you have natural strengths that I see all the time—and I think this could make you even better."

She'd compliment the best, see the best, and yet encourage growth in others.

Laura, a director under Hayworth for multiple years, conveyed the same sentiment. Like Dan, she was regularly challenged by Kim ("I always got the sense from them that Kim and her team saw more in me than I saw in myself") but felt cared for in the process. The strong rapport that Hayworth cultivated went a long way in making that possible:

> Kim always had an open-door policy. You knew that a light rap on the door was all it took to step in and have a conversation with her. She made it clear that people were her job.

> Nothing was more important to her than her people. The work for her *was* her people. And that's amazing because she still got so much done.

After speaking with Dan and Laura, I asked Kim directly about her leadership style and learned that her approach was a conscious choice based on her beliefs about the importance of humility. She describes her philosophy this way:

> In a time where leadership is so often described as being assertive and powerful, humility is not sexy at all. But it is the way to lift everybody up. [Humility means] I don't come across as the superstar or the person who has all the answers. Suddenly everyone feels like they were a part of the solution, not just the few who are confident and articulate and willing to speak up.

> It's not flashy or what's portrayed in media today, but it's the hidden sleeper of leadership.

The result of Kim's high competence and high character was commitment from her team. Laura said simply, "I respect her and I want to do my best work for her." Dan similarly said, "You definitely didn't want to disappoint her….it helped me to work harder, not just to get the job done, but to please her. To make her look good." Kim's humble leadership created an enjoyable atmosphere for her employees to work in and engaged their hearts and minds in a powerful way.

***

Kim's example shows that humble leaders engage their people better for several reasons. Because they create more authentic connections with their followers, humble leaders generate more personal commitment to organizational goals. Because they normalize failure as part of the path to growth, team members are more resilient in the face of challenges and stay engaged even when obstacles arise. And since humble leaders appreciate others' strengths and contributions, their followers get to do their best work every day, further increasing each team member's investment in their own work.

Research by Gallup (the pioneer of CliftonStrengths and the strengths-based philosophy) found the average leader only engages about 34% of their people at any given point in time. Sadly, that means that two-thirds of the American workforce falls somewhere between doing the bare minimum at work and actively checked out—shopping online, searching for other jobs, or even working a side hustle while on the clock.

Alarmingly, the results are even worse when managers focus exclusively on improving their employees' weaknesses. These leaders only get high energy and performance out of *2%* of their workforce. Yes, you read that right. Leaders who focus on fault-finding disengage 98% of their teams!

Left unchanged, this process creates a vicious cycle where the leader becomes angrier and more despondent. Imagine being a leader who feels you are surrounded by incompetent people. No matter how often you address problems, the people never get any better and you end up doing all their work. The next week, you experience the same issue again, and the pile of problems has grown. Despite your best efforts to hold others accountable, you feel like Sisyphus, eternally rolling the same boulder up the same hill.

In contrast, leaders who found creative ways to leverage their team members' strengths engaged a whopping *67%* of their people—twice the level of the typical manager and light-years ahead of the weakness-focused leaders. Individuals led by strengths-focused managers feel understood and valued by their bosses, in turn creating deeper trust and organizational commitment. And because they get to use their strengths every day and contribute meaningfully, they tend to get energized by challenges rather than demoralized, leading them to persist through difficult circumstances and deliver their best work.

Rich Sheridan, CEO of Menlo Innovations in Ann Arbor, Michigan, has found normalizing failure provides another lever to boost engagement. He encourages his employees to "run the experiment" when they have a new idea. When one of his team members was struggling to find childcare for her new infant, Sheridan said, "Bring her in!" When the woman was skeptical that her three-month-old child could coexist with a bunch of software developers sitting in cubicles in a technology company, Sheridan said, "Let's try it before we defeat it." His persistence prevailed, and she ran the experiment to see what would happen. It turns out the baby did fine, as did her mom. The experiment was a success, and that child opened the door for dozens more to follow.

> *Leaders who built on others' strengths engaged 67% of their people. Managers who focused on weaknesses only engaged 2%.*

While humble leaders undoubtedly have a wide range of views on children in the workplace, the mindset of "running the experiment" remains consistent. As people who embrace a growth mindset, they know failure and learning are foundational to success. Consequently, humble leaders give their team members permission to take risks and try new things. Sheridan was not only able to keep this new mom employed at Menlo, but he communicated to others in the company that he was humble enough to question the status quo and potentially be wrong. As a result, leaders like Sheridan get more energy, investment, and commitment from their people.

Organizational outcome #2: Results

It was a Wednesday morning in early 2018, and Mark Cuban had a problem. On any other day in February, the billionaire entrepreneur, *Shark Tank* star, and Dallas Mavericks owner probably would have been focused on the record of his beloved basketball team. However, their performance on the court was the least of his problems at the moment. Instead, Cuban was preoccupied by a breaking *Sports Illustrated* investigation that revealed his Mavericks possessed one of the most toxic cultures in the NBA.

For years, executives and staff within his organization had been harassing or assaulting women with little to no retribution. The misogyny was rampant, making the overall organizational culture "corrosive." And to make matters even worse, his team was on its way to finishing a lowly 13th in the Western Conference. So Cuban picked up the phone to call Cynt Marshall.

As Mavericks fans would soon learn, Cynthia Marshall was a powerhouse leader. A trailblazer from Day 1, she had been the first Black senior class president of her San Francisco Bay Area school, the first Black cheerleader at UC-Berkeley, and the first Black woman to serve in an executive officer position at AT&T. After several decades of service at the telecommunications giant and a strong track record of cultural transformation, she was now semi-retired and consulting with companies on issues of organizational culture.

The morning Cuban called was a busy one for her, so it took her husband's insistence to get her on the phone. "Mark Cuban has been trying to reach you. You need to call him back," he urged her.

"Mark who?" she replied. As a busy executive and mother of four children, Marshall had little time to give to reality TV shows, so she didn't recognize the billionaire's name. But once her husband explained who Cuban was, Marshall agreed to return his call.

Two days later, Cuban announced Marshall as the Mavericks' new interim CEO. Marshall shared that her goal would be to transform the ball club's toxic culture into an exemplar for the rest of the league. She planned to execute 200 initiatives in her first 100 days. Beginning with an individual 1:1 listening session with every Mavericks employee, Marshall would dive headlong into getting to know her new organization and industry. Sporting the leadership mantra "Every voice matters. Everybody belongs," Marshall went about driving cultural transformation through a radical commitment to getting all voices to the table.

The Dallas Mavericks soon did just that, reshaping an executive leadership team that had been all White men into one that now included women and people of color. She fully eliminated the gender pay gap within the organization and also recruited the team's first female assistant coach. And she formed an advisory council of leaders in the community to "tell me the things that I don't want to hear" as they sought to better serve the Dallas-Fort Worth metroplex.

While Marshall's plan was full of to-do items, it was also high on values. Character, Respect, Authenticity, Fairness, Teamwork, and Safety (physical and psychological) soon became the team's primary playbook. CRAFTS—one of the many acronyms or alliterations Marshall lives her life by—would form the basis of the new culture. She promised these values would "not just be on the walls, but in the halls. We make every decision with these values." True to her word, Marshall soon began to act on those principles.

As a result of her efforts, the toxic culture that afflicted the Mavericks has been all but eradicated. An organization that was perceived at the bottom of the league for its unhealthy culture has now won two straight Inclusion Leadership Awards from the NBA. And along the way, her team happened to climb from a 24-win season and 13th-place finish to a 52-win record and third-place finish overall.

It's clear to see that Marshall is a champion of diversity, equity, and inclusion, but her story also reveals that she embodies the four elements of humble leadership. First, while anyone could have spotted the obvious hole in her résumé— her most recent sports experience was college cheerleading— Marshall frequently goes one step further to openly discuss her failures, limitations, and vulnerability. Whether it's a serious story about her battle with colon cancer or a lighthearted anecdote about walking out of the house in just her slip, Marshall demonstrates her accurate self-awareness through self-deprecating stories. But her self-perception also includes a clear awareness of her own strengths. She recognized she had much to learn from Cuban about the NBA, but she also stood confidently on her proven ability to lead cultural transformation. This accurate assessment of her strengths and weaknesses provides the artful blend of confidence and approachability that distinguishes her leadership.

Second, her appreciation of others' strengths and contributions was at the heart of her drive for inclusion. Just as Collins advises in *Good to Great,* her first step was to "get the right people on the bus and in the right seats," then learn from them where the organization needed to go. Her "every voice matters" mantra thus provides far more than a feel-good story about racial and gender equity; it offers a strategic advantage.

Third, she embodies a growth mindset in the way she approaches her own learning curve and in the expectations she sets for others. Where some CEOs place the most importance on performance, Marshall instead values authenticity, even when it's imperfect:

> I don't want [our people] to feel like they have to go into a phone booth (if they can find one these days), put on a cape with a big M on their chest for Mavs, and come in as some superhero. We're all the same.

I want the people who get up out of bed in the morning—the baggage they have, the cultures they have, the good things, the great things that they have, the experiences, the beliefs, the philosophies. That is what needs to walk in our doors because we're all different. That's what will help us make great decisions and tap into different cultures and do well as a business and do well as a country.

Marshall's emphasis on authenticity enables her employees to bring their quirky strengths to work and frees them to be honest about their limitations so they can grow.

Finally, Marshall's greater purposes play a significant role in her leadership as well. Her passion for diversity, equity, and inclusion is obvious based on the strategic priorities she embraces, and her frequent role as a barrier-breaker motivates her to do a good job "for the sisterhood." But at an even more fundamental level, love for others drives her:

I believe as a leader, there are three things that I really need to do listen to our people, learn from our people, and love our people. It's important for me to truly, truly love them as people, not just as employees.

Marshall's purpose is not just self-advancement or top-line revenue growth; it's caring deeply for every person she is responsible for as CEO. It is this deep love for her people that creates the psychological safety and strong relationships needed to get the best investment from each of her team members. And as her organization's cultural transformation demonstrates and winning record reinforces, her humble approach to these daunting challenges is truly driving performance within her organization.

***

As research shows, Cynt Marshall is not the only humble leader to outperform her competitors. In 2015, researchers Amy Ou, David Waldman, and Suzanne Peterson set out to discover whether humble CEOs produced more financial value for their companies than their less-humble peers. To answer their question, the research team put 105 technology firms and their top managers under a proverbial microscope over multiple years. To ensure their results were accurate, the researchers measured everything from the CEO's humility to their educational background, tenure with the organization, and even their level of charisma. After controlling for all these variables, what they found confirmed their hypothesis: companies led by humble CEOs generated significantly better financial returns than companies led by non-humble leaders.

But why?

The fundamental mechanism driving much of their success was a decision-making process called "balanced processing." Because these humble leaders were able to keep their own egos in check, junior leaders could challenge their boss's ideas and flush out inaccurate assumptions. This healthy conflict meant that everyone's preconceptions got challenged—even the CEO's. The resultant ideological debate meant multiple strategic pathways could be considered, not just the ideas of the most powerful people. This process of setting politics and power aside to do what was best for the company as a whole led these teams to make better strategic decisions and produce stronger financial performance over the long haul.

As Marshall's story demonstrates and research further validates, choosing a humble approach elevates an organization to new heights.

Organizational outcome #3: Contagious humility

In late 2014, video surfaced of a strange interaction on a crowded subway somewhere in Belgium. During an otherwise normal commute, a passenger named Geert Van De Vijver started chuckling at a funny video on his iPad. Standing alone with his head down and headphones in, the bald, middle-aged man with a day-old beard was engrossed in something hilarious on his device. His unusual behavior elicited raised eyebrows and curious glances from passengers nearby. But he didn't notice. Instead, he just kept on laughing—his body shaking with gasps and snorts as he guffawed at his screen.

Soon, his fellow commuters couldn't suppress their own smiles. Despite not seeing what he was watching, they too began to laugh—mouths covered, eyebrows raised, looks of surprise and joy splashed across their faces. The stranger's laughter had spread to a dozen people in less than 90 seconds.

It turns out the incident was not a coincidence but a clever stunt from a Belgian ad agency. Van De Vijver—a professional "laughter coach"—had been planted on the train to show the power of social contagion. Following his performance, undercover coworkers on the train revealed themselves and handed out cans of Coke and postcards with a smile on them. "Happiness starts with a smile" read the closing script of the commercial.

***

Following the COVID-19 pandemic that shut down the world in 2020, we hardly need reminders that contagion is powerful. Even still, many leaders do not understand how infectious their own attitudes are. Research by Brad Owens and David Hekman finds that humble leadership itself is highly contagious. The two researchers interviewed dozens of individuals to understand what it was like to work for a humble leader, and what they found was powerful. Because humble leaders are aware of their own shortcomings, admit their mistakes, and model teachability, others around them begin to believe that mistakes are a normal part of life. As one individual expressed it, these leaders convey "it is okay to be a 'work in progress' here."

But far from allowing the team to settle for mediocrity, the people led by humble leaders embrace the growth mindset, own up to their mistakes, and push themselves to get better.

Amazingly, humility rubs off on others, creating a culture where people become more open to feedback and more transparent with their shortcomings. When this effect begins to take hold, an individual attribute (growth mindset) begins to take root at the organizational level, leading entire teams, divisions, or organizations to become more adaptable and innovative. In both laboratory and field experiments, the researchers found the higher the humility of the team's leader, the higher that team's collective humility was as well. The result was quicker organizational learning and stronger results overall.

I observed this powerful contagion effect in action when completing my dissertation research. A friend of mine told me about a small and little-known college that had gone from the brink of closure a few years prior to being more financially viable and affordable for students at the same time. The college had been losing market share for years only to have matters get significantly worse during the Great Recession. But somehow, just a few years later, the institution was not just surviving but thriving. The turnaround seemed miraculous, and remarkably fast. Since very few colleges become more affordable over time, I was curious about what they did. And since rapid change within higher education is just as rare, I was even more curious about how they did it.

During my investigation, I discovered the catalyst: two humble leaders within the organization. One was Ron Everly, the quiet and mild-mannered president; the other was Bill Jameson, a brilliant and dynamic provost. Together, they had set out to reinvent the college's strategy to prevent it from closing. Doing so required a vigorous financial analysis of each of the institution's programs to see which ones would be viable long-term and which others needed serious attention. To execute the analysis, Jameson suggested some evaluation criteria, selected the faculty and staff for the committee, and let them get to work.

Most colleges conduct these analyses from time to time—especially when budgets are tight—but this one was different.

Unlike the program reviews that occur behind closed doors, the college's leadership decided they would openly post the unvarnished report for all faculty and staff members to see. Every department could now see the profit generated by each of their colleagues and compare it to their own. While this move would be a bit unusual for the typical for-profit entity, it was downright shocking within the ivory tower of higher education. But senior leaders wanted not just to raise awareness of the serious financial issues the institution was facing but also to communicate that they deeply trusted their colleagues by sharing this information.

Finally, after collecting all the data, the committee sat down to distill its recommendations for the senior leaders. After reviewing the numbers, one of the committee members, a computer science professor, spoke up and made a shocking recommendation: his department should be eliminated. The performance data were simply irrefutable. If the college was going to continue to operate and fulfill its mission, he could no longer justify his own department.

I was amazed when I heard this story. The act of selflessness would have been shocking at any of the organizations I'd worked at. I needed to know *why*. What would cause someone to sacrifice their own livelihood for the sake of their employer?

As I asked faculty and staff members these questions, the word *humility* kept rising to the surface. Humility was a value in their religious tradition, and it was a value their president had embodied over three decades of service at the institution—first as a professor, then as the chief leader. For years, the college's leader had been modeling the openness and teachability that so many of the faculty and staff members now practiced themselves.

Even the program review process itself showed their humble leadership. The provost had the self-awareness to know he needed to create an independent committee to study the issues lest he be perceived as meddling. By entrusting his colleagues with the authority to do the study (then sharing the data openly with the rest of the organization), he showed respect for their capabilities and trustworthiness. The fact that leaders took an analytical approach in the first place showed their growth mindset—they didn't prematurely assume they knew where the problems were. And it was their greater purpose of sustaining the institution and serving students that enabled them to make difficult sacrifices in the change process.

Humble leaders within this small college didn't appear by accident. They were the natural by-product of working in a humble culture and under a humble leader for several years. Fortunately for them, it was this humility that enabled them to make the tough decisions needed to survive and thrive as an organization.

Conclusion

As research shows, becoming a humbler leader doesn't just increase your happiness, strengthen your relationships, and boost your own performance—it also has a marked impact on the people around you. Humble leadership is contagious, spreading across entire teams and cultures, fostering the learning cultures that most of us long to work for. And for the more financially-minded of us, it also produces fantastic results—not just in the incredible case of Microsoft, but also in the Dallas Mavericks, Seattle Seahawks, and various colleges and universities.

Each of the leaders described in this book brought their own unique spin to humble leadership. Satya Nadella's humility expresses itself through his relentless curiosity and empathy. Cynt Marshall embodies a transparency and sense of humor that makes her approachable and charming. Pete Carroll's most notable traits are his positivity and energy level. But despite the differences in their personalities, humble leadership provides a common foundation for their success: an operating system of sorts that enables their uniqueness to be expressed effectively and get fantastic results.

***

These incredible results raise some questions. How can we all become humbler leaders? How does that process unfold?

Surprisingly, the book that propelled humble leadership into the limelight doesn't offer much in the way of solutions. When Jim Collins was asked, "Can you learn to become Level 5?" Collins admitted, "I still do not know the answer to that question. Our research, frankly, did not delve into how Level 5 leaders come to be, nor did we attempt to explain or codify the nature of their emotional lives." He goes on:

> We would love to be able to give you a list of steps for getting to Level 5—other than contracting cancer, going through a religious conversion, or getting different parents—but we have no solid research data that would support a credible list. Our research exposed Level 5 as a key component inside the black box of what it takes to shift a company from good to great. Yet inside that black box is another—the inner development of a person to Level 5 leadership. We could speculate on what that inner box might hold, but it would mostly be just that, speculation.

Collins declined to guess as to what a path toward humble leadership might look like because he had no data on it at the time. Like the humble leaders he wrote about, he recognized his own limitations and stuck to his data and expertise as a business strategist, not a leadership coach.

While few can match Collins' insight on business development, his silence leaves us with questions about the next stage leadership development. Excellent books like *The Ideal Team Player* by Patrick Lencioni likewise champion humble leadership but offer relatively little guidance for developing this trait. In a nutshell, that is why I wrote this book: to pick up the conversation where Collins and Lencioni left off so you can take the next step on your journey toward humbler leadership. While I'll likely never match the business acumen or research prowess that Collins brings to his studies of organizational change, I have dedicated years of my life to studying how personal leadership change works. This unique perspective will hopefully infuse some valuable insight into this topic and move the conversation forward.

In the next two sections, we'll leave behind the *why* of humble leadership and explore the *what* and the *how*. Specifically, what does humble leadership look like in practice, and how can we become better at it? But before jumping to the 10 mental mindsets and skillsets that can help you become humbler, we first need to answer a fundamental question: How do people change?

Spoiler alert: being a humble leader is not a matter of undergoing an existential transformation overnight. It's a simple process of doing and becoming, doing and becoming.

Part 2:

How Personal Change Happens

5

The Do-Become Flywheel

In Part 1, we discussed the "What?" and "So what?" of humble leadership. Here we turn to the next stage: "Now what?" What can you do to become a humbler leader?

Bridging the "Transformation Gap"

To be fair, this is no small challenge. Becoming a humbler leader goes far beyond adopting a new leadership technique or conversational approach. True change happens at a fundamental level—the core beliefs and practices that form your identity—and this kind of change is rare. After all, each of us has walked away from insightful books, engaging conversations, or enlightening presentations with the thought, "Wow, that really changed me!" only to find two weeks later that nothing is any different. The truth is that the gap between *inspiration* and *transformation* is huge—a deep, yawning chasm.

So how do we bridge the Transformation Gap? That is the question that drives Part 2 of this book. In this section, we'll explore a handful of mindsets and skillsets that can help you become a humbler leader. But before launching into those specific strategies, it's worth stepping back to consider how purposeful personal transformation takes place.

What follows may be the least exciting insight of the entire book, but I'm convinced it's true: moving from *inspiration* to *transformation* requires *application*.

In other words, *do the work*.

Rocket science, right?

The Transformation Gap

Inspiration   **Transformation**

(deep yawning chasm)

As self-evident as this statement is, application (i.e., real, sustained effort) is rare. We shouldn't be surprised, though. After all, application requires work—mundane, slow, consistent work. Who wants to volunteer for that?

Inspiration, on the other hand, is invigorating. Those lightbulb moments are the mental equivalent of cotton candy for your brain. Exciting new ideas create a surge of energy in your body in much the same way pure sugar does when it dissolves on your tongue. But just as you cannot live on sugar alone, inspiration by itself doesn't lead to lasting change. You've got to do the work.

Cathexis

But what does "doing the work" mean in this context? The psychological idea of *cathexis* (kuh-THEK-sis) offers some helpful framing here. Coined by the psychoanalyst Sigmund Freud in the early 1900s, cathexis is the amount of mental or emotional energy you invest into something. For your own development purposes, think of it in two dimensions: consistency, and intensity. By both intensely and consistently applying an idea, you'll begin to transform.

You instinctively get this idea, I'm sure. If you want to go from your couch to a 5k, you know waking up the morning

The Application Bridge

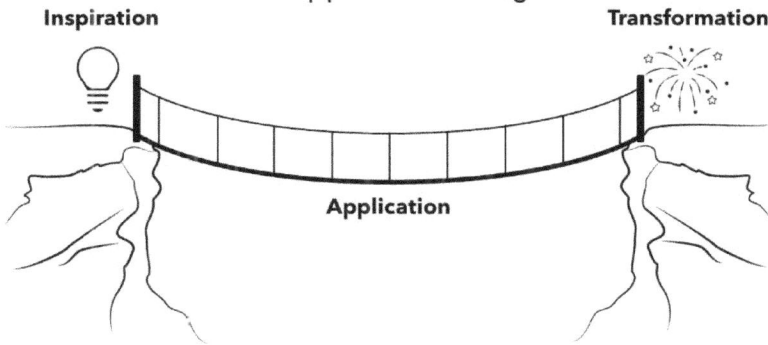

before the race and trying to sprint 3.1 miles for the first time is a recipe for failure. Intensity alone will burn you out.

Similarly, you understand that simply taking the stairs a few times a week is not enough to build the stamina you need. Consistency without intensity leaves you unchallenged. That's why basically every race preparation plan combines intensity and consistency. You need both to transform flabby muscles into those of a runner.

This is obviously far easier said than done. After all, if it were easy, everyone would be doing it. But if most people fail to transform themselves through conscious effort, why should you be any different? And if major personal change is what we're after, where do we start?

> *Cathexis: The consistency and intensity of energy you invest into something.*

You become what you do...

The answer to these questions lies in another concept of human development that is hidden in plain sight. I call it the *Do-Become Flywheel.*

If you've ever used a training plan to prepare for a race, you probably noticed something right away: the intensity demanded on Day 1 was far different from Day 21. While you only walked a mile on your first training day, you ran it a week later. In these plans, intensity is variable; it ratchets up over time.

On the other hand, consistency is usually...well, consistent. Except for planned recovery periods, your plan probably had you exercising every single day. That consistency enabled you to get into a predictable rhythm, forming a cornerstone habit you could build on. By the end of your training program, an exercise that seemed impossibly intense a few weeks prior is now feasible (albeit still challenging) because of your consistent and intensifying effort.

The great news is that your leadership development follows a parallel path. In essence, radical transformation does not require radical transformation. Reinventing yourself as a humbler, more purposeful, more effective leader doesn't require you to quit your job, move to Nepal, and meditate for 12 hours a day. Instead, evolution steadily unfolds as you faithfully and consistently apply a few key ideas. Leadership development, like any lifelong pursuit of real value, is "a long obedience in the same direction," to borrow from the philosopher Friedrich Nietzsche. Those minor changes build with compound interest over time, slowly morphing you into the kind of person you want to be.

> *Radical transformation does not require radical transformation.*

These repeated behaviors not only become part of your routine, but *who you are* at a fundamental level. As philosopher Will Durant simply states, "We are what we repeatedly do. Excellence, then, is not an act, but a habit."

Author James Clear builds on this idea, fleshing out the process in his bestselling book *Atomic Habits:*

> The more you repeat a behavior, the more you reinforce the identity associated with that behavior. In fact, the word *identity* was originally derived from the Latin word *essentitas*, which means *being*, and *identidem*, which means *repeatedly*. Your identity is literally your "repeated beingness."

He continues:

> Every action you take is a vote for the type of person you wish to become. No single instance will transform your beliefs, but as the votes build up, so does the evidence of your new identity....
>
> It is a simple two-step process:
> 1. Decide the type of person you want to be.
> 2. Prove it to yourself with small wins.

These "votes" for your identity build up over time. In the process, they not only rewrite your narrative about who you are, but they also begin to change your neurologically hardwired responses to situations.

This naturally occurring process plays out in many different dimensions of life. After weeks of counseling and being more present with your spouse, you stop seeing yourself as someone who's bad at relationships and start seeing yourself as someone who fights for a good marriage. After saying "no" repeatedly to new obligations, your identity as a people-pleaser begins to give way to a new identity—someone who has healthy boundaries and avoids over-commitment. And after months of looking for ways to serve your team instead of advancing your own agenda, you begin to feel more like the humble leader you aspire to be. As you do the things you need to do, you become the person you want to become.

> *Leadership development, like any lifelong pursuit of real value, is "a long obedience in the same direction."*

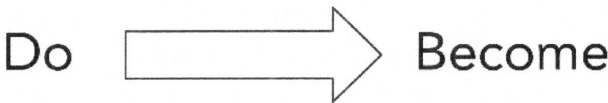

Do ⟹ Become

The Do-Become Flywheel

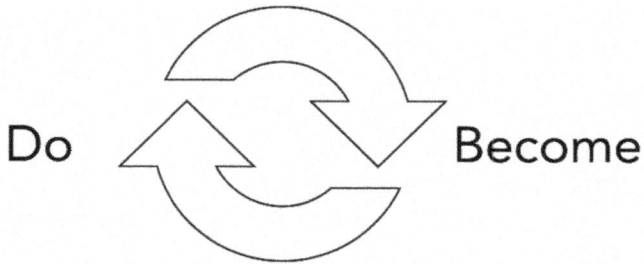

Do · Become

But this process does not simply work in one direction. As your identity changes and you become the person you want to be, you also begin to naturally do more of the things you want to do. Your actions continue to shape your identity, but now your identity also shapes your actions. Who you have become—or who you are striving to become—now drives what you do.

...and who you're becoming drives what you do

The result is what I call the *Do-Become Flywheel*. Flywheels are large, weighty discs used in machines to conserve momentum. While these simple inventions often take a great deal of effort to get turning, they conserve energy so efficiently that they almost become self-propagating. Collins popularized the concept with business leaders by arguing that great companies build momentum in flywheel fashion, consistently taking small actions that each turn the wheel of progress forward one more rotation. Like snowballs rolling down a hill, they grow more powerful with each tiny snowflake that adds to their momentum.

I've experienced the effect of flywheels in my own life several times over, whether in silly things or serious ones. I pride myself on taking care of my sleep needs, for instance. Unlike many of my peers, I started going to bed early in high school. I maintained the habit in college and beyond, gradually moving my bedtime up earlier and earlier. Now I'm in bed by 9:30 almost every night, and I love it. Eight hours of sleep is my personal secret to success in life.

What's notable about this habit for me is the amount of effort it takes: none. I don't have to make a nightly decision about my bedtime; it's already been decided. I don't have to wage an internal battle to go to sleep early; I look forward to it. Sure, I have to say "no" to late-night commitments to make it work, and it took extensive discussions with my wife to convince her that the cool kids go to bed early, but this part of my identity is now so innate that it takes no energy to maintain it. In short, my consistent choices have so thoroughly shaped my identity that my behavior now flows effortlessly out of it.

This process of identity-shaping behavior doesn't just work for well-established identities, though; it also works for identities that are still being developed. I'm currently on this journey with generosity, for instance.

For years, I wanted to be a generous person. Most of the people I admired were generous with their time and money, and that value was a core tenet of my own faith as well. I wanted to embody that virtue, but it was so hard for me. Our budget was always tight while I was growing up, and over the years, I had come to believe I needed to hoard everything I had for the future lest I be found wanting down the road. Consequently, my scarcity mindset caused me real pain when I needed to let go of my possessions.

One day, I finally decided to just start giving more money away. I knew it would never be easy for me, but I was also convinced it was the right thing to do. So I increased the amount we regularly gave to our church and to other charities. The leap was scary, but it felt good. I knew I was becoming more of the person I wanted to be.

Then one day, I was confronted with my own inconsistency in a small but convicting way. We were having some friends over for dinner that night, and I spent hours smoking a brisket in preparation. As I was stowing away the succulent leftovers after dinner, a thought occurred to me: *I should offer to send some food home with them. I love it when my friends do that.* The generous thought made me feel good, so I turned to head back to the dining room to extend the offer.

But then I hesitated. The voice of scarcity piped up: *But... what about those brisket sandwiches I was planning to eat for lunch tomorrow?....And the brisket nachos I was going to make for dinner?....And wouldn't brisket mac and cheese just be amazing?* Suddenly, I felt stuck. As the two competing narratives played out in my head, I stood staring off into space in the kitchen trying to figure out what to do.

I had the right to keep the meat, of course. *I've already given so much away,* I thought. *No one would expect me to offer any more.* And that was true.

But in that moment of hesitation, I thought back to my commitment toward generosity. Unlike the financial commitments I had made, I didn't have an objective goal of a certain percentage of food to give away. The decision fell in a gray area. But I did have an aspirational identity to use as a lens in this situation. In those few seconds, I asked myself, *What would a generous person do?* and the answer was clear: send them home with lunch for tomorrow.

In that moment, I decided to *pretend* to be that generous person. It still felt somewhat unnatural, and the internal debate still murmured on. But I knew by placing another vote for that aspirational identity, I took one step closer to becoming the person I wanted to be. By faking it, I would eventually make it.

It's a small and silly instance, I know. But that thought process demonstrates how *who we want to become* informs *what we should do.*

If your kids are underfoot in the kitchen and you're about to snap, don't ask, "Do they deserve it?" but "What would a kind parent do?"

When the cashier gives you back too much change, instead of asking, "Will they miss it?" ask, "What would a person of integrity do?"

When you're called out rudely for something that wasn't your fault...or when a colleague is dominating a conversation…or when your team isn't hitting their goals, ask yourself, "What would a humble leader do?"

We aren't limited to making choices based on our past identities; we can embrace the identities we want to embody and make our behavioral decisions accordingly. As novelist Kurt Vonnegut said, "We are what we pretend to be, so we must be careful about what we pretend to be." Or as the martial artist/sales jackhammer/agri-tourism entrepreneur Dwight Schrute said:

Before I do anything, I ask myself, *Would an idiot do that?* and if the answer is *Yes*, I do not do that thing.

For centuries, humans have chosen these aspirational identities based on their religious or communal values. Faith traditions created an entire genre of literature devoted to telling tales of the saints so that we could model our lives after them. But in today's irreligious and independent Western world, the decision of who we will become now rests on our own shoulders.

If we decide not to choose an aspirational identity for ourselves, we will default to the identities that our culture and social circle define for us. On the other hand, if we plot an intentional course for ourselves, this vision of the good life places guardrails around our behaviors. The behaviors we choose as a result reinforce those identities, and our identities in turn naturally direct our future actions.

By embodying an identity that is not yet natural for us, we gradually incorporate this new identity into our lives. In other words, by choosing to "fake it," we slowly begin to "make it."

Building desire

One other by-product of the Do-Become Flywheel is a change in *desire*. One of my recent clients experienced this firsthand on his journey of living more purposefully. Craig woke up one day in his early forties and realized he was drifting in life—not being intentional about exercise, finances, personal growth, or planning the next steps in his career. After trying but failing to solve the problem on his own, he sought out a coach because he was now serious about changing his behavior.

In one of our first coaching sessions, Craig identified one reason he struggled to sustain change: he really didn't *want* to change. He didn't want to work out—he *wanted to want to work out*. His desire wasn't there, so going through the motions of working out felt both inauthentic and unreasonably difficult.

Craig's dilemma is common to us all. But the good news is a lack of desire does not have to equate to a lack of change. As Craig soon discovered, *desire does not have to precede behavior.* If you want to become the kind of person who works out daily, you don't start by hyping yourself up to believe cardio sounds fun. That would be lying to yourself, and that sham will fall apart after your first workout. Waiting for the I-love-every-second-of-this kind of desire before beginning simply means you'll never begin.

So if desire isn't a prerequisite for change, what is? As Craig discovered, *willingness*, not desire, is the starting place. If I'm willing to take the right steps, play along, and see how it turns out, then over time I discover something magical: what I *do* shapes what I *want*. My behavior not only shapes my identity, it also re-forms my desires.

> My behavior not only shapes my identity, it also re-forms my desires.

I'm sure you already know this. Once you began running regularly, you started to miss it when your schedule didn't allow it. After eating vegetarian for months, you noticed how sluggish your body felt after a burger. And while it felt impossible to read for more than five minutes at a time a few months ago, now you crave curling up with a good book at the end of your day.

Desire does not have to precede behavior. *Behavior can lead to desire.* If you have a *willingness* to start, an *openness* to change, a *curiosity* about how life could be different, the desire can follow.

When Craig came to this realization, it was like a weight was lifted off his shoulders. He didn't have to beat himself up any longer for disliking what he was doing. Going from no exercise to regular workouts was simply going to be a grind, full stop. By accepting that reality, he suddenly stopped pressuring himself to enjoy the experience and could instead just focus on showing up to do the work.

Ironically, a few weeks in, Craig's desire started to change. A few weeks into trying on these habits, his new lifestyle started to fit and feel better. His desires shifted from actively disliking his new rhythms to feeling neutral about them. Eventually, he even started to crave them at times.

After two months of slowly increasing his intensity and consistency in these domains, he began to feel natural desire. He articulated it this way:

> For the first initial push of the boulder, I needed someone to push it with me. Now that it's rolling, it would feel more strange to go backward now.

> Normally after having a setback, I would have beat myself up and feel defeated. Now, I want to get back to doing it. I've felt the goodness of what it does, and I want to continue that.

Notably, Craig's efforts weren't perfect. He had slips and failures along the way. But what was different this time was his change in identity. Rather than spiraling after a setback and succumbing to the idea he was a poser, he began to embrace his identity as someone who lives intentionally. By continuing to put in the work after failures, he cast more votes for his new identity. The congruence he experienced between his values and his actions felt good, and now the thought of living with any less integrity sounds strange to him.

As Craig's example shows, the great news about the Do-Become Flywheel is that doing the right thing becomes *easier* over time. As Stanford neurobiologist Carla Shatz summarizes, "Cells that fire together, wire together." When we repeat patterns of thought or behavior, our brains hardwire those paths in, stamping the process into our bodies.

So what does all this mean for you? Well, if your Do-Become Flywheel is already turning in the direction of humble leadership, that's great! Hopefully this book enables you to accelerate the flywheel even more on your path to becoming a humbler leader. And if your loop is inert or turning in the wrong direction, the remainder of this book will show you how to exert force in the right direction to help turn any vicious cycles into virtuous ones.

Conclusion

Transformation takes a lot of personal investment over an extended period of time. After all, if it were easy, we'd all be perfect. But as daunting as it may be to consider how much work true transformation takes, there's also something refreshing about this dose of reality: deep personal change is within your grasp. The personal actualization we want is not limited to people who can afford high-priced conferences, have connections to amazing mentors, or have the budget to hire an executive coach. Change is within our reach if we're willing to do the work.

By consistently taking small steps to build positive momentum, you begin to craft a new identity that slowly perpetuates itself. You too can make the jump—or more accurately, the steady march—from inspiration to transformation. When applied to your character and leadership, that means you can gradually but steadily become the humbler person you intend to be.

But what does that require in practice? How do you know what to do when? It starts with having the right plan.

6

Making a Plan for a Change

In Chapter 2, I asked a rhetorical question: Why doesn't every leader have "Become a humbler leader" as the primary goal on their leadership development plans? This question assumes, of course, that you have a plan to develop your leadership. My experience has shown very few people do, however.

Building a development plan is one of the simplest and most essential action items you could take away from this book. After all, if you're inspired by the concepts and stories shared here but don't channel that motivation into a plan of action, in two weeks, little will have changed for you. I don't want that to be your fate, so let's explore how to build a plan.

But first, a little context on how development planning works.

A brief history of the modern personal development plan

Most of us know planning is important. We've heard the pithy phase attributed to Benjamin Franklin, "If you fail to plan, you plan to fail." Although Franklin never uttered these words (Reverend H. K. Williams did in 1919), he's an understandable candidate for the quote. The great-great-grandfather of the American self-help movement made plans for lots of things, including his own moral development.

Franklin describes this plan in his autobiography:

It was about this time I conceived the bold and arduous project of arriving at moral perfection. I wished to live without committing any fault at any time; I would conquer all that either natural inclination, custom, or company might lead me into....

But I soon found I had undertaken a task of more difficulty than I had imagined. While my care was employed in guarding against one fault, I was often surprised by another....

I concluded, at length...that the contrary habits must be broken, and good ones acquired and established, before we can have any dependence on a steady, uniform rectitude of conduct.

For this purpose, I therefore contrived the following method.

As Franklin describes, he determined to take his character formation seriously. He identified 13 timeless virtues he wanted to cultivate, then built a schedule to do so. His plan was to focus on one virtue at a time for one week, then move onto the next virtue the subsequent week. After 13 weeks, he would start at the top of his list again, enabling him to hit every virtue four times a year (13 weeks x 4 cycles = 52 weeks). And the final virtue on his list? Humility.

Adding the 13th virtue to the list in the first place was itself an act of humility. As he describes, it wasn't his idea originally:

My list of virtues contained at first but twelve; but a Quaker friend having kindly informed me that I was generally thought proud; that my pride showed itself frequently in conversation; that I was not content with being in the right when discussing any point, but was overbearing, and rather insolent, of which he convinced me by mentioning several instances; I determined endeavoring to cure myself, if I could, of this vice or folly among the rest, and I added *Humility* to my list...

Franklin's plan was straightforward, giving him a column for each day of the week and a row for each of the 13 virtues. Upon daily examination, Franklin would make a mark for every time that day he had failed to practice the virtue of emphasis for that week.

As Franklin described, his efforts to grow in humility worked. Despite being surprised by the volume of his faults initially, he soon found that by softening his language and listening to others more intentionally, he became more persuasive and less adversarial. Although he himself acknowledged he still fell short of "moral perfection," he did find it became more natural for him over time.

If this focus on virtue management sounds quaint, it unfortunately is. As the cultural commentator David Brooks argues in *The Road to Character,* American culture lost its focus on character development over the last half century—especially the pursuit of humility. For example, only one of President Eisenhower's 23 cabinet members went on to write a memoir about his government service (which occurred in the 1950s). A mere three decades later, 12 of President Reagan's 30 cabinet members would go on to do the same. While there's certainly nothing wrong with writing a memoir, this anecdote embodies the shift our culture has undergone over the last several decades. Today's emphasis on personal brand management reflects larger societal trends, such as increases in narcissism and self-centeredness scores on longitudinal studies. Similarly, the average American teenager is much more likely to aspire to be famous now than to pursue public service. Celebrity has become our substitute for character or true significance.

While some culture values may have declined since Franklin, our methods for creating personal change have improved. The rare individuals today who are working on strengthening their inner core don't have to rely on daily self-accountability alone. Experts in learning and development have been building on Franklin's method for the last 300 years. In the process, they've designed frameworks that incorporate the guidance, social support, and additional tools most of us need to accelerate our growth. The best-known of those frameworks is what's called "the 70:20:10 rule."

A modern approach: The 70:20:10 rule

In the mid-1980s, Morgan McCall, Michael Lombardo, and Ann Morrison wanted to know how leaders learned on the job. Once they were out of school and working in management positions, how did they stay sharp? Through interviews with 191 successful executives, they found leaders tended to put their learning into one of three buckets:

1. **Formal learning**, which includes classes, books, podcasts, and TED Talks
2. **Social learning**, which could be thought of as mentors, coaches, bosses, and colleagues
3. **Experiential learning**, which includes on-the-job application and practicing skills

Since their findings, many learning and development professionals have used these same buckets when building leadership development plans with their team members. Although the labels for each bucket may differ from organization to organization, this rough framework has endured due to its combination of simplicity and breadth.

This overarching schema is helpful, but how much time and energy do you allocate to each area?

For folks who go straight to college after high school and then enter the work force, the preparation for our first job looks something like this:

- **70 percent** of our time and energy is invested in **formal** learning: taking classes, studying for standardized tests, sitting for professional exams, etc.

- **20 percent** of our time and energy is invested in **social** learning: learning from the boss, meeting with mentors, asking peers for advice, etc.
- **10 percent** of our time and energy is invested in **experiential** learning: volunteering, internships, etc.

This ratio is helpful for equipping new leaders with the basic context and concepts they will need to succeed as individual contributors. If I'm hiring an electrical engineer, for instance, I hope they spent enough time in class to learn the difference between amperage and voltage. Likewise, I wouldn't want my kids attending a school where the teachers skipped the formal learning of college because "they're just naturally really good with kids" and didn't think they needed to learn child development principles. Spending most of our time in formal learning makes a lot of sense early in life when we don't yet have the knowledge or skills to contribute much in professional settings.

But as McCall and colleagues found in their research, most of their successful executives reversed the ratio in this way once they hit the workplace:

- 70 percent **experiential** learning
- 20 percent **social** learning
- 10 percent **formal** learning

Once leaders had built a foundation of knowledge from their years of formal learning, most of their ongoing growth came in the form of application on the job. Formal learning still provided valuable frameworks, concepts, and schemas, but it was the ongoing implementation of those ideas that took their skills to the next level.

Consider a manager who wants to develop her coaching skills. She knows her people have more to offer, but she isn't sure how to draw it out. She's tried a lot of different things but finds herself working harder and getting diminishing returns.

Then one day, she stumbles across some research that says that employees want more coaching from their managers and that organizations with coaching cultures outperform their competitors (which is true). So she decides to go all in and add coaching skills to her leadership toolbelt. What would be the optimum approach for her?

1. Just start coaching without any preparation.
2. Study how other leaders coach their direct reports.
3. Read the five bestselling books on coaching.

By now, you know that while any of these approaches would lead to some improvement, the best approach would be a blend of the experiential, social, and formal. If I were designing a training regimen for this manager, it would look something like this:

- **Formal learning** (3 hours, or 10 percent): Training on the philosophy and practices of a coach.
- **Social learning** (6 hours, or 20 percent): Learning from experienced coaches through observation and by getting coached personally.
- **Experiential learning** (21 hours, or 70 percent): Practicing coaching and reflecting on the process.

While the hypothetical plan outlined here follows the 70:20:10 rule, there's nothing magical about the specific proportions of the framework. In fact, since the debut of the 70:20:10 rule decades ago, research continues to fine-tune the ideal. One such study from the leadership development firm DDI found most leaders actually use a 55:25:20 split between the three areas. Regardless of whether the ratio between experiential and formal learning is 2:1 or 7:1, the core message is clear: leaders need to invest significantly more time in applying ideas than in simply learning them.

Put simply, they need to do the work.

But what exactly does "doing the work" look like? Beyond these broad buckets of activities, what does it take to build an effective strategy for your growth? As you work to chart your own path toward becoming a humbler leader, ensure it contains all four elements of a solid plan.

#1. A good plan starts with a clear goal

First, a good plan begins with a clear goal. Having a clear goal tells you what's important and what's not, provides the foundation for accountability, and increases your chances of success.

Knowing what's important is critical because it keeps you from writing someone else's plan. I've worked with plenty of leaders who have unsuspectingly fallen into this trap. During a review of their leadership competency assessment, we'll often have a conversation like this:

> *Leaders need to invest significantly more time in applying ideas than in simply learning them.*

Client: "I really want to get better at entrepreneurial thinking."
Me: "Okay. What makes that important to you?"
Client: "Well, it's my lowest score."
Me: "Right. And how important is entrepreneurial thinking to your current role?"
Client: [pause] "Not at all. I don't have any chance to do this in my job."
Me: "Okay. And what about the next role you want? How important would it be for that job?"
Client: [longer pause] "Probably not important at all. [pause] I guess I just don't like seeing that low score on my report, so I want to get better at it. [pause] But now that I think about it, there are a lot of other skills that are more important for me."
Me: "Great. Let's dig into that list."

Stepping back to clarify your goal ensures you prioritize the activities that will best help you accomplish that goal. In this client's case, their goal was success in their current role, then a promotion. Taking time to clarify your goals in this way prevents you from living someone else's life or pursuing someone else's idea of success. Without this step, you may wake up one day and question why you're running so hard on the hamster wheel of life—obtaining "success" but little satisfaction. If this happens to you, it might be because you are pursuing someone else's goal.

A clear goal helps you prioritize, but it also provides accountability. After all, if you don't have a clear goal for your development, you don't have true accountability because you'll never know whether you're making progress or not. And if you don't have accountability to yourself or to others, odds are this priority will fade from your radar when life gets busy or seasons change.

Maybe you would say you are not a "goal person"—that goals aren't motivating to you or you don't want to be held accountable to some arbitrary standard. I get that. But every one of us operates from goals, even if they're subconscious. We all have a vision—clearly defined or not—of the future we're working toward. Some of us just write that vision down, or make a vision board, or put metrics and timelines and resources around it. So the question isn't "Will you *set* goals?" but "Will you *clarify* and *commit* to your goals?"

If you do commit to a clear goal, the goal-setting science shows you are more likely to act and find success. Researchers at the University of Scranton found that people who consciously committed to their New Year's resolutions were 11 times more likely to achieve them than people who identified a problem they needed to change but stopped short of declaring their goal. As simple as it sounds, just saying, "I'm going to get better at _____ over the next _____ months" already increases your odds of success.

> *The question isn't "Will you set goals?" but "Will you clarify and commit to your goals?"*

To set those clear goals, "begin with the end in mind," as the leadership sage Stephen R. Covey says. When you look back on today a year from now, what will you wish you had focused on? As you think about the future you want for yourself, your team, and your family, what's on that list? Until you can get specific about what you want, you won't know how to get there and you won't be motivated to change. It's the stark discrepancy between our present and intended states that catalyzes action, so taking time to analyze that gap is critical.

At a more fundamental level, though, it's helpful to ask yourself, "What do I *really* want?" Would gaining that promotion really make you happy long-term? Or is your deeper desire to know you're doing a good job and a promotion just serves as an indicator that you are valued? Understanding your desires at this deep level will help you aim at the right target.

Lastly, don't just think about what you want to accomplish; think about who you want to become. When you're lying on your death bed and looking back over your life, what kind of legacy do you want to have left behind? If you were able to attend your own funeral, what do you hope your family and friends would say about you? Odds are, the stories they will tell will be much more about your character than your accomplishments. Hopefully, humility is one of those character traits.

#2. A good plan has clear and concrete action items

The next step in formulating a good plan is crafting specific action items. It's one thing to say, "I want to become a humbler leader," or "I want to better understand my strengths," but until that goal has clear action around it, it's not real. It's not real because you won't know what you need to do.

If you don't know what you need to do, odds are the high motivation you feel right now will slowly fizzle in the face of the ambiguity. If you want to become a clearer communicator but don't know what to do to make that happen, it's unlikely you will spend a lot of focused time working on that skill. Stay long enough in that state of arrested progress, and eventually much of that energy may sour into disappointment over your lack of momentum.

As coaches often say, "clarity brings energy." Taking time to clearly map out these steps will increase your chances of success exponentially and motivate you to get started right away.

This was one of the most surprising dynamics I noticed when I first started coaching. I remember ending my first coaching call with a young leader named Samantha. Sam had several health problems that were making her lethargic on the job and at home. She was determined to turn around her poor physical wellness so she could be more productive and effective.

On that first call, she created a lengthy list of action items she wanted to achieve that month: set new goals for herself, start meal prepping so she'd eat healthier, establish a new gym routine, and more. I felt nervous for her because I knew taking action on this list would require a significant change in her behavior. She had been trying to improve in this area of life for months but hadn't made any substantive progress. What made her think she could suddenly do it now? Were we just setting her up for failure and disappointment?

To help her guard against overcommitting herself and falling short, I asked, "How do you feel about this list?" Her response was instantaneous. "I feel great!" she said. "It's so energizing seeing everything written out like this. I know what I need to do now, and I can't wait to get started."

On our next call a month later, I was eager to hear how things had progressed. As I'd suspected, the list proved to be a bit too much. She thought more about her goals and did get back to the gym, but she hadn't started meal prepping as planned. As she reflected on what she'd done, she felt some disappointment about coming up short.

"It's understandable that you're disappointed you didn't achieve all your goals," I said. "But let's think about this in comparison to what you were doing before. How often were you going to the gym before our first call?"

"Not at all," she said, a smile slowly starting to spread across her face. "That's true—I have made a lot of progress actually." Her energy began to visibly increase as she realized she was creating momentum for the first time in a long time. And as we continued to work together over the next few months, that early momentum would prove to be critical. She soon established a daily workout routine that kept her sane during many ups and downs of her personal life—all because she took the time to clearly map out her next steps.

As you work to craft your own clear and concrete action items, ask yourself: Do I know exactly what I need to do? Have I clearly scripted the next step? Is it clear enough that I will know whether I did it or not?

Let's say the next step in your humble leadership development plan is becoming a Multiplier (Chapter 16). Consider how effective these three different action items would be in advancing that goal:

1. **Good action item**: Try not to offer my opinion so much in my team meeting.
2. **Better action item**: Instead of just sharing my opinion, I'll try to convert 80% of my insights into questions at my team meeting.
3. **Best action item**: Before each team meeting, I'll set aside 10 minutes to strategize about how to draw out the unique insights of my team through open-ended questions. Then I'll ask those questions.

See the difference? Version #3 is not only more objective (making it harder to fudge an answer when asked how successful you were at it), but it's also more actionable. If I see a meeting coming up on my calendar, the event prompts me to block off 10 minutes to complete this step. This concrete clarity will lead me to do it more consistently and make me more effective when I do it.

Although every good action item will be clear and concrete, the approach beyond that varies. Some action items are preplanned (e.g., "I will run every morning before work so I can compete in a half-marathon next fall"), while others are reactive (e.g., "Any time someone is speaking to me, I will put away my technology and make eye contact the entire time"). Some focus on a one-time activity (e.g., "Read a book on emotional intelligence"), but others target a new habit with a trigger, routine, and reward (e.g., "Before I leave my office for the day, I will take a deep breath and clear my head. Then I'll go home and hug my family"). Regardless of the approach you choose, clarity is paramount.

#3. A good plan aligns resources

After you've set a clear goal and a concrete action item, the next phase in creating an effective plan is aligning resources. By ensuring you have the time, budget, and expertise needed to successfully complete your action items, you show that this plan is indeed a priority to you. This step alone removes a significant barrier to your success.

Connecting resources to your plan communicates to yourself and others that you are serious about your commitment. While this outcome may not seem essential at first glance, the gravity is quickly felt when it's absent.

Perhaps you've seen this gap between priorities and resources in your own organization at times. Your leaders say employee development is important, and yet there is no budget allocated to it, no point person owning it, and no time dedicated to it. Their words say one thing but their resource allocations say another. The discrepancy reveals a disconnect between their espoused values and their actual values. They talk the talk, but they don't walk the walk.

The same is true for you. If you have a goal but you're not dedicating resources to pursue it, you've created the adult equivalent of a Christmas list for Santa Claus. You've laid out your wishes and are now praying they magically appear some distant morning. But hope is not a strategy, and a wish list is not a plan. If this is truly a priority for you, you need a plan that integrates resources to support your goals.

Once you do identify and secure the resources you need, you create a second positive outcome: a greater chance of success. Consider these two different plans for the same goal (from Chapter 11). Which one is more likely to succeed?

Goal: Get better at listening actively to others.

Plan #1

o Close my computer and put away my phone when someone is speaking to me.
o Try not to interrupt people when they speak.

Plan #2

o Close my computer and put away my phone when someone is speaking to me.
o When someone else is speaking, wait three seconds before responding so I don't interrupt them.
o Share this goal with my boss and ask her to hold me accountable to it in our 1:1s.
o Read *The Coaching Habit* by Michael Bungay Stanier to learn more about good listening.
o Create silence breaks in my day so I feel less hurried.

What differences do you notice? Besides being much more robust, Plan #2 has some other significant advantages over Plan #1. While both are aimed at the same goal, the second plan assumes you'll need to create additional margin in your life to change your course. It also recognizes you'll need help from outside yourself in the form of accountability and insight to be successful. By taking time to thoughtfully connect these resources to your plan, you stack the deck in your favor.

So how can you ensure you have the right kind of resources for your plan? First, think creatively about the full range of resources you could access. Resources come in various forms: peers, managers, skilled professionals, previously-developed frameworks, financial support, or additional time away from your job. Anything that can increase your odds of success is a potential resource. One of the most critical resources for your success is accountability from others, which I'll discuss more in Chapter 12. No matter what your goal is, odds are that some person or organization out there can help you accelerate your success.

If you have a goal but you're not dedicating resources to pursue it, you've created the adult equivalent of a Christmas list for Santa Claus.

So before diving into do the work yourself, stop and ask, "Who else can help with this?" Rather than trying to assess your strengths on your own, who could speak truth into your life as a mentor? Instead of doing a self-study on goal-setting, what courses does your employer offer? Yes, you could pay for coaching out of your own pocket, but can you find some professional development funds to make this easier? Broadening your horizons in this way increases your chances of success and encourages you to appreciate others' strengths and contributions, deepening your humility along the way.

#4. A good plan builds over time

Lastly, a good plan builds on itself one step at a time. As we discussed in the previous chapter, you'll be much more successful if you can effectively manage your cathexis over time, slowly building up momentum to tackle harder challenges as you grow. Treat it like eating an elephant: one bite at a time.

To help you craft a development plan that effectively builds in intensity and complexity, the final section of the book lays out 10 practices with detailed key actions that will help you become a humbler leader. This section flows a bit differently than the previous two sections, as this list functions more like a menu of options for you to consider than a linear process. Rather than prescribe a one-size-fits-all approach for your growth in humility, I've chosen to offer a range of activities that have worked for me and my clients so you can build a learning plan that meets your specific needs. Consequently, these practices are organized by the pillar of humble leadership that they address most directly, enabling you to skip to the domains that you most need to focus on.

Because of this different layout, I'd suggest you read these chapters differently than the prior ones. This encyclopedia of humble leadership practices may be daunting to consume all at once, but it's proven valuable for other readers as a reference guide. And when you're ready to try one of the practices, you'll notice that each chapter ends with a *"Humbler* in Two Minutes" box—a simple suggestion for how to implement these ideas to become humbler in two minutes or less. These prompts can help you simplify the complexity of the chapter and start making progress immediately.

Many of these practices are simple—some even glaringly obvious. While I wish I could tell you there are some novel concepts here that no one in the history of humankind has ever unearthed before, the truth is many of these practices are hundreds of years old. Most of them you probably already know to be important. My aim is not to reinvent the wheel of humble leadership but to consolidate a wealth of proven insight into a practical and actionable format you can implement today.

Even though many of these practices will already be familiar to you, I'd wager you're not actively prioritizing most of these mindsets or skills. Most of the leaders I coach are busy fighting the daily whirlwind and neglect the fundamentals of leadership in the process. My goal here is to help you understand the fundamentals in a new light while rallying you to apply them in a more focused way. If you accept that reminder and respond with action, I promise you'll see results as your Do-Become Flywheel turns and your momentum builds.

Online resources

To help you pull all this advice together into a coherent plan, I've included three development-planning templates on my website for your use.

The first is geared toward skill acquisition and uses the 70:20:10 rule as a framework. This is your standard leadership development plan.

The second is a daily habit planner. Rather than providing overarching guidance for your development, this one focuses on how to make specific behaviors more regular for you.

The third is a legacy planner. This is the most unorthodox of the three but potentially the most meaningful. I was inspired to develop this planner years ago when reading *Next Generation Leader* from the pastor and leadership expert Andy Stanley. In it, Stanley argues that "your natural talent will eventually outstrip and outpace your character if you do not develop a parallel track upon which to run." It revealed that while I had plenty of plans for my career, I had none for my character or legacy. What daily or weekly habits was I engaging in that would ensure others remembered me as a humble, wise, and loving person? This plan was an attempt to answer that question. If you also felt pricked by the questions about your future legacy, this planner is for you.

Before moving on to the next section, I'd encourage you to stop and reflect on your goals. You'll have the greatest clarity about what to "order" off the menu of development options if you've decided in advance what you want to accomplish. That said, if you're still unsure of what you want, you may find that the 10 practices outlined in the ensuing chapters speak to you differently and help you clarify what it is you most want. Regardless of whether you stop to plan now or wait until later, you'll hopefully find the development templates helpful.

To be clear, there's nothing sacred about any of these templates; the goal is just to provide clarity, commitment, and accountability. Regardless of which one you land on, pick something that works for you, and use it. I guarantee you'll get further than you would without one.

You can find those resources at JoshWymore.com/ humbler or by using the QR code here.

Conclusion

If you want to give yourself the best chance to become a better leader, take a page from Ben Franklin and make a plan. By finding the optimal blend of experience, social support, and new frameworks, you'll ensure your goals actually get traction. And when you take the time to craft a clear goal, design concrete action steps, pull in the right resources, and build practices that increase in intensity and consistency over time, you'll find yourself enjoying progress soon.

Part 3:

Ten Practices to Become A Humbler Leader

Pillar #1:

Cultivate an Accurate Self-Perception

7

Increase Self-Awareness

Since the foundation of humble leadership is an accurate self-assessment, it makes sense that we would start with this fundamental question: how can we gain more self-awareness?

It's worth tackling self-awareness head-on because it is a notoriously slippery thing to grab ahold of, especially if you don't already have it. Individuals who lack self-awareness often have a tough time accepting feedback, fail to empathize with others' perspectives, and shirk ownership of their mistakes.

As harmful as these practices are themselves, the most damaging impact is a continued lack of self-awareness. If I refuse to believe my boss's critical assessment of my performance, for instance, I have eliminated the possibility that I'll ever understand my blind spots.

Unfortunately, these problems are all too common. Organizational psychologist Tasha Eurich's research shows that while 95% of people think they're self-aware, less than 15% actually are. Most frighteningly, senior leaders are significantly less likely than entry-level leaders to have an accurate view of themselves. Because of their track records of success and limited exposure to people who will speak truth to power, many executives have disproportionately high evaluations of their own emotional intelligence.

So if self-awareness is both critical and difficult to attain, how do we get more of it? Perhaps the best way to kickstart the process is by understanding the Johari Window.

The Johari Window

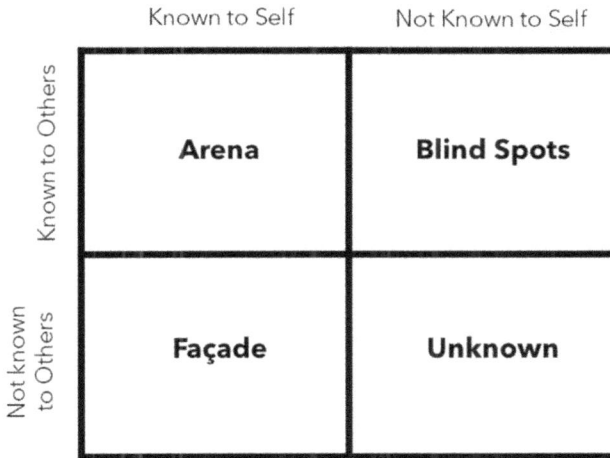

	Known to Self	Not Known to Self
Known to Others	Arena	Blind Spots
Not known to Others	Façade	Unknown

Developed by two psychologists in the 1950s (Joseph Luft and Harrington Ingham—i.e., Jo-Hari), the image captures the four dimensions of information about ourselves:

1. **Arena**: Knowledge that is out in the open and shared by everyone.
2. **Blind Spot**: Knowledge known by others about me, but not known by me.
3. **Façade**: Knowledge I know about myself but have not shared with others.
4. **Unknown**: Knowledge about myself that none of us have at the moment.

While the two quadrants on the left represent things we know fully about ourselves, the rightmost quadrants are invisible to us. Sometimes these knowledge gaps are harmless, but at other times, they can be derailers. These unknown areas cause the biggest threat to our own self-awareness.

I coached a leader who had several of these knowledge gaps, and a few of them were serious. In our first conversation,

I asked him to tell me about his strengths and weaknesses. He confidently ran through a long list of strengths, but then hit a dead end with his weaknesses. "You know…I've never thought about that.…I can't think of any weaknesses," he replied. That was a first for me! I smiled and nodded, trying to hide my combination of surprise and disbelief. *At least he's being honest!* I thought.

Twenty minutes later, he now had something to add to that list. During our conversation we were reviewing the results of a leadership assessment he completed, and he was perplexed by some low scores he had received in his interpersonal domain. "Ok, Josh—this doesn't make sense. I'm in sales, and I do relationships for a living. So I don't really understand why I got low scores for managing relationships," he protested. I explained how the rating system worked, then asked him to consider several behaviors that seemed to share a common theme. He paused, and a look of concern spread across his face. "Wait, is this saying that I'm only nice to people if I need something from them?" he asked.

I smiled. "That's a great question," I responded. "What do you think?"

I won't repeat the expletive he used then, but suffice it to say, he was not pleased to learn about this potential weakness. A characteristic that had been previously unknown to him was now evident, and he had to decide how to respond. To his credit, he didn't reject or explain away the insight; he rebounded quickly and approached the challenge with the same commitment to getting results that had enabled him to become one of the top-performing sales leaders at his company. Our conversation opened up his Johari Window a bit more, and the new insight provided him with the opportunity to become a better salesperson—and human being.

Blind spots like these are common for all of us; we'll never have a totally objective view of ourselves. But by engaging in productive introspection and seeking outside feedback, we can protect ourselves from needless risk and give ourselves more control over our futures.

So what can you do to expand your own self-awareness? Here are a few suggestions to get you started.

Utilize assessments

Perhaps the easiest and least vulnerable way to fast-forward your self-awareness is completing a personality or behavioral assessment. Designed to tell you things about yourself you might not already know, a good assessment can be a powerful tool in understanding your impact on others, tendencies under stress, and even hidden motivations. I'm a big fan of a good assessment, though not all assessments are created equally. Here are a few I use with my clients regularly:

- **Livstyle**: Useful for its comprehensiveness, this tool is a DISC (Dominance, Influence, Steadiness, and Conscientiousness), conflict management, and MBTI (Myers-Briggs Typology Indicator) assessment all in one. (http://findyourlivstyle.com/)
- **CliftonStrengths**: Designed to identify your top five latent talents, giving you greater awareness of your natural strengths. (https://www.gallup.com/cliftonstrengths)
- **Enneagram**: Because this assessment speaks to your fears and motivations more than your behaviors, this assessment is great at uncovering Quadrant 4 (the dimension unknown to you and to others). (https://tests.enneagraminstitute.com)
- **DDI's leadership assessments**: These business simulations stand apart from the rest by evaluating your behaviors and leadership competencies, not just your personality tendencies. By observing how you solve leadership challenges when under stress, the assessment moves beyond predicting what you *might* do to showing what you *actually* do as a leader. (https://www.ddiworld.com/solutions/leadership-assessment)

- **360 feedback**: If your company offers 360-degree feedback, this can be a gold mine—though the data is sometimes tough to swallow. If they don't offer it, consider working with a consultant to implement a fair and well-designed one. These data are best at addressing the Blind Spots.

The above assessments are great for general self-awareness, but for a clearer line of sight on humility more specifically, these two tests can be beneficial:

- **Humility**: See the self-assessment on my website (JoshWymore.com/humbler). And if you're really brave, ask someone else to complete it about you and share their scores.
- **Narcissism**: If you think you might be on the overconfident end of the spectrum, the official Narcissism Personality Index (NPI) is enlightening. It's designed to measure clinical (i.e., very high) levels of narcissism, but its insights can be useful regardless. (https://openpsychometrics.org/tests/ NPI/)

Regardless of which assessments you choose, thoughtfully considering the results from any of them will increase the accuracy of your self-perception and strengthen the foundation you need for humble leadership.

Read insightful books

Books are amazing because they open up entirely new worlds of thoughts and emotions to you from the comfort of your couch or earphones. For self-awareness in particular, this diversity of experiences is helpful because a good book can describe things about you that you didn't even know.

Some books that have increased my self-awareness the most are nonfiction books that address it head-on (like *Leadership and Self-Deception*), but I also find I resonate with great biographies (*Hamilton*) or novels (*Crime and Punishment*) as well. Some of these stories are powerful because they energize my imagination with a vivid picture of humble leadership, and these images are essential for informing how I should show up as a leader. But others are simply helpful because they're honest about the human condition. (For a full list of book recommendations to help advance your humble leadership, see JoshWymore.com/humbler.)

Regardless of what you're reading, find something that speaks to you and ask yourself "Why? What is it in me that connects so deeply to this character or idea?" If you get angry every time a deadbeat dad is mentioned, what does that say about your own views of your dad or thoughts about your own parenting? If you're inspired by leaders who sacrificed greatly, what motive is that stirring in you, and why? These questions lead to the last action step you can use to drive up your self-awareness.

Reflect

For any change in your self-awareness to take place, conscious reflection must be at the heart of it. To paraphrase the famed educator John Dewey, we don't learn from experience; we learn from reflecting on experience. I'm sure you know some people who have 10 years of leadership experience and others with one year of experience they've repeated 10 times without change. The latter encounters the same problems repeatedly yet somehow fails to learn anything. Without reflection to understand the situation and chart a new course, nothing ever changes.

> *We don't learn from experience; we learn from reflecting on experience.*

Reflection can take on various forms. I'm a big believer in journaling since it gives me a chance to think with my fingers and see my thoughts on a page, thus creating some healthy, objective distance. While most faithful journalers I know use paper and pencil, I'm a digital guy. I love being able to write faster, avoid hand cramps, and search back through old journal entries. In the last two years, I've added 127,000 words to that document, making it twice as long as this book! Keeping these records of my thought processes provides the added benefit of revisiting my thinking later to see how my perspectives have changed (or not). Both realizations can be humbling.

I'm also a verbal processor, so I appreciate the opportunity to reflect alongside friends, bouncing my hypotheses off them and refining them together. As a coach, I have the privilege of doing this everyday with leaders, and what never ceases to amaze me is how many insights they have during our conversation just because they're taking time to slow down and reflect. Nine times out of 10, it's their thoughtful consideration that turns on a lightbulb for them, not my insightful question or keen observation. This pattern tells me many leaders have pent-up reflection waiting to spill out if they will only step back and ask themselves some questions.

However you choose to reflect, ensure you're asking the important questions. By asking the important questions, I mean getting to the heart of the matter: your motives, emotions, values, and thought processes. When deciding on whether to pursue a promotion, for instance, spend less time thinking about the title and pay and more time asking yourself questions like:

- What are my competing motivations here?
- What is my first instinct?
- What values am I trying to maximize?

Similarly, when preparing for a difficult conversation with someone who's hurt you, focus less on what the other person did to frustrate you and think more about which of your values or assumptions were violated. Of all the things in life you could get upset about, why this? What does your offense say about your priorities and thought processes? And are your priorities and thought processes aligned with who you want to be? How you proceed in this moment determines whether your

Do-Become Flywheel turns forward in the direction of your growth or slows down. By "paying attention to the tension," as Andy Stanley says, we'll gain much greater insight into who we are and create greater alignment with our intended identities.

Many leaders have pent-up reflection waiting to spill out if they will only step back and ask themselves some questions.

Taking time to reflect on our motives, values, and experiences helps us become humbler by illuminating our biases, subjectivity, and limitations. Grappling with our flawed assumptions and mixed motives reminds us that our perspective is neither wholly pure nor absolutely objective. As a result, we become more open to other perspectives on ourselves and the world.

Humbler in Two Minutes

- **Utilize assessments.** Take the free humility assessment at JoshWymore.com/humbler
- **Read insightful books.** Reflect on your favorite movie or book character. What is it that you resonate with so much?
- **Reflect.** Describe a decision you wrestled with recently. What made it so challenging for you?

8

Embrace the Humility Paradox

At the center of humility is an apparent paradox—two seemingly contradictory realities that are simultaneously true. On one hand, humble leaders are constantly aware of their limitations and mixed motives. At the same time, they also seem gracious, present, and peaceful. How do these two mindsets cohabitate?

The truth is humility not only appears as a paradox but *must* be a paradox. In fact, it's the healthy tension between these extremes of scrutiny and gratitude that creates humility itself.

Going on a journey of humility is akin to two hikers taking divergent paths at the same time. One takes the road over the mountain peak, while the other descends into the valley. As they both follow their own path, the distance between them grows. Similarly, embracing the Humility Paradox is like walking two paths at once. By deepening your awareness of your gifts on one hand and your shortcomings on the other, your sense of humility expands.

Here's how this process works for me:

I often start or end my days by evaluating the depth of my shortcomings on the previous day. Where did I blow it or come up short? What do I need to confess? Who might I need to apologize to? This daily examination process raises my self-awareness, helps me correct mistakes that need to be mended, and prevents me from repeating harmful patterns again the next day.

But perhaps most importantly, it's humbling. When I recognize the depth of my shortcomings—the selfish choices,

The Humility Paradox

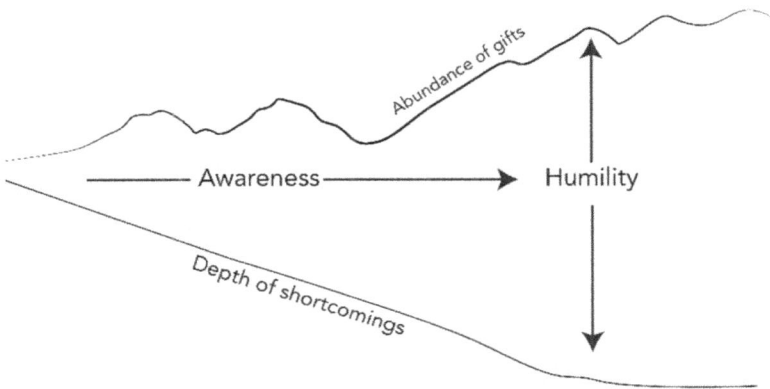

limited knowledge, and pervasive brokenness that is baked into the human condition—I realize I have a lot to learn. I imagine how difficult it must be to live or work with me at times. I grapple with my smallness in the universe. And I am reminded how much I need the wisdom, grace, accountability, and support of others.

At this juncture, I can go in one of two directions. If my reflection stops here, my conclusion is that I'm small, finite, and somewhat helpless. Coming eye to eye with my flaws can create feelings of shame, inadequacy, or anxiety. Left unchecked, this thinking can even result in depression.

But if I continue in my reflection and shift to gratitude for the abundance of my gifts, the outcome is wholly different. My awareness of my need for others doesn't end in a cul-de-sac of despair but instead turns to thankfulness for the gifts I've received:

- A wife who loves me despite my self-centeredness
- A community that sharpens my thinking
- A job that lets me use my strengths to make a difference in the lives of leaders while providing for my family

The list goes on and on, including some things I've earned through hard work and some things that are pure acts of mercy. When I meditate on these things, my natural response is gratitude for others, kindness to myself, and graciousness when I encounter my equally-flawed fellow human beings.

Just as a singular focus on my failures can lead to despair, thinking only of my gifts can lead to arrogance. The truth is, if I don't understand the severity of my shortcomings, I can't truly appreciate the blessings I've received. If I'm only viewing my highlight reel, I'll start to think my wife is lucky to be married to me, my friends are privileged to be in my presence, and all my work accomplishments are proof of the innate brilliance I bring to the world. Because a gift isn't a gift if I think I've earned it, I stop feeling blessed and start feeling entitled.

> *Just as a singular focus on my failures can lead to despair, thinking only of my gifts can lead to arrogance.*

In short, I need to explore both extremes of the paradox to cultivate humility in myself—and the further I go down each path, the greater my capacity for humility.

How can you tell if you need to spend more time in the humility paradox? For me, the trigger is a creeping sense of superiority. On the continuum of "I'm worthless" to "I'm the best thing since sliced bread," I personally tend to suffer most from big-headedness. I show up as overly confident in my own abilities and less interested in others' contributions. Any time I catch myself walking into a meeting thinking, *I have a lot of good insights to offer here*, that's a sign I may be mistaking my confidence for competence.

The truth is I do have something to offer—*but so does everyone else.* If I take time to reflect on my own shortcomings, I recognize that I'm not better than anyone else—and at the

The Four Quadrants of the Humility Paradox

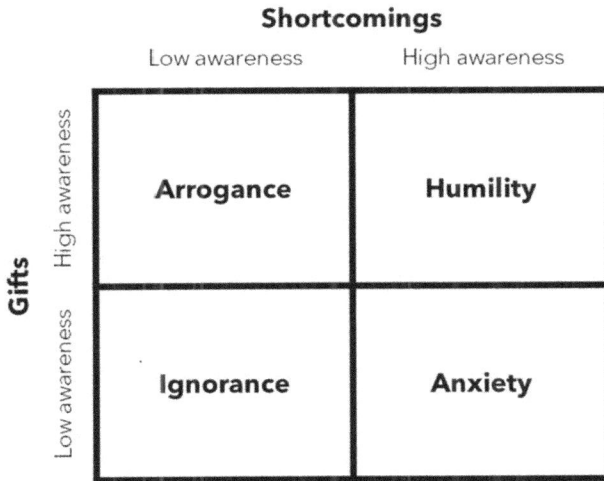

Shortcomings

	Low awareness	High awareness
High awareness	Arrogance	Humility
Low awareness	Ignorance	Anxiety

(left axis label: **Gifts** — High awareness / Low awareness)

same time, no one is better than me. I have inherent worth, but I'm not flawless. I'm secure, but I'm not superior. Holding these two realities in tension helps me close my mouth and open my ears, which is no small accomplishment for me.

Here is one practical way you can embrace the Humility Paradox.

Establish a daily habit

Making this process a part of your daily rhythm will significantly increase its effectiveness, as your perspective does not have time to drift too far off-course. Whether you choose to begin your morning with this routine, wrap up your day with it, or find some other time in-between, you'll get the most benefit from this practice when it's done regularly. I personally enjoy starting my days off this way, and I also take time with my daughter each night to reflect together on what we're grateful for. Both are great bookends to my day.

> *A gift isn't a gift if I think I've earned it.*

If you decide to go this route, consider using the free Daily Habit Planner (JoshWymore.com/humbler) to map out how you'd like to institute this practice. Expect some trial and error in finding the right time, place, and method, and know that the practice may feel a little forced at first. I started journaling off and on in college, yet it's taken me almost two decades to decide to make it into a daily practice. But now that it's a part of my morning routine, I crave it if it doesn't happen.

As you establish this daily habit, you'll find yourself becoming humbler as you continually anchor yourself to deep truth. Reflecting on both the brokenness and beauty in your life helps you understand yourself in right relationship to the universe while cultivating greater reliance on the gifts of others as well. Both of those movements strengthen your humility.

Humbler in Two Minutes

- **Establish a daily habit.** Schedule a consistent time to reflect on the highlight of your day and the greatest disappointment you experienced.

9

Practice Metacognition

Metacognition is the practice of "thinking about our thinking," or stepping back to consider how we're processing information (*meta* = higher, so literally "higher-level thinking"). As we work to channel our thinking toward more productive aims, understanding our current state is essential before we can move forward. But more fundamentally, thinking about our thinking helps us with the first element of humility: an accurate assessment of our own strengths and weaknesses. Becoming increasingly mindful of how we think heightens our self-awareness and makes us more cognizant of our shortcomings.

The reason metacognition awakens us to our limitations is that serious self-scrutiny reveals dozens of cognitive biases at play in our lives every day. These blind spots are everywhere, far beyond the realm of what we typically think of when we talk about biases (i.e., race- or gender-based discrimination). As mountains of social science evidence now show, our thoughts and behaviors are not as logical and systematic as we would like to think. We frequently respond intuitively or emotionally to rational questions and trick ourselves into believing we arrived at our conclusions based on thoughtful consideration. Consequently, we place too much confidence in our poorly-conceived judgments, resist correction from others, and make systematic mistakes.

Here are a few of my favorite cognitive biases:

- **Fundamental Attribution Error**. Attributing others' flaws to their character and your own mistakes to extenuating circumstances. *Example: He was speeding because he's a jerk; I was speeding because I'm late for an important meeting at work.*
- **Confirmation bias**. Seeking information that reinforces existing beliefs rather than challenging your perspective. *Example: When weighing whether you should make a large purchase, you search for positive product reviews rather than critical ones to make yourself feel better about the choice you really want to make.*
- **Halo effect**. Giving undue positive credit to someone based on positive attributes in another area. *Example: Agreeing with someone's rationale because you perceive he or she to be attractive or charismatic.*
- **Recency bias**. Skewing your assessment of a situation in favor of recent events or memories. *Example: Unconsciously biasing an annual performance evaluation based on last month's positive or negative performance rather than considering the year as a whole.*
- **Negativity bias**. Weighing negative information more strongly than positive information. *Example: Remembering your day as a failure because of one bad thing that occurred.*
- **Anchoring bias**. Giving disproportionate weight to the first piece of information you encounter. *Example: Viewing a pricing markdown as a bargain because it is considerably less than the original (but highly inflated) sale price.*

If your goal is to become a humbler leader, awareness of your own cognitive limitations should lead you to question yourself and invite others into the decision-making process. In doing so, you engage others in meaningful ways, grow by learning from them, and ultimately make better decisions.

Thinking about our thinking goes beyond understanding our biases. It uncovers unproductive patterns and false assumptions, too. Unfortunately, this is an experience I have all too often.

On one recent Saturday, I was making soup to take to a sick friend when my wife mentioned that the bathroom floor was ready to be scrubbed. We'd had a plumber come by the day before to unclog our toilet, and for some reason, a smell of sewage persisted after he'd left. While she wasn't explicitly asking me to do the cleaning, I decided to take a break from cooking and handle the bathroom myself.

An hour later, the project I thought would be quick was dragging on. My best efforts to eradicate the sewage smell were unsuccessful. Now, my meal would be done later than planned, meaning our entire morning of errands was also delayed. I hate being late, so irritation and frustration naturally started building inside me as I felt resentment for how Emily's project had derailed my plans.

My crankiness grew throughout the day as one project begat another and another. What should have been a quick floor mopping turned into me removing our toilet to replace the wax ring at the base, then repeating the floor cleaning once more. All this was occurring during the time I'd planned to watch my beloved Texas Longhorns play. I was intermittently irritable for the next 24 hours, huffing and sighing in my passive-aggressive way because I felt like I was on a hamster wheel of home projects.

It wasn't until I sat down and started journaling the next day that I realized the flawed assumption I had made: *Emily never asked me to clean the bathroom*. My cavalcade of bitterness was all based on the premise that my wife had turned my plans upside down and stolen control of my weekend. But that was patently false. *I* decided to clean the bathroom; *I* decided to take on the next project; *I* even decided when our errands should be, so the fact that I was "running late" was itself a construct of my own thinking. A few false thoughts, left uncorrected, led to a scuffle that soured my weekend and dampened my relationship with my wife.

What's the point here? The point is our Enlightenment-loving Western world idolizes controlling our emotions, *but we also need to control our thoughts*. No part of our humanity is perfect; each aspect of our life is flawed or limited in some way. Our thinking—logical and balanced as it may sometimes be—is far from error-free. The sooner we embrace this truth, the sooner we can begin to get better at separating fact from fiction.

Here's how to use the process of metacognition to increase your self-awareness and humility at the same time.

State your assumptions

Even if our thinking is logical and objective, we'll make inaccurate decisions if that logic is built on flawed assumptions. If you are an entrepreneur who wrongly assumes dial-up internet is making a comeback, no amount of hustle or savvy marketing can make up for that fundamentally wrong assumption. The same inherent limitations hold for the strategic or tactical decisions we each make every day in leadership.

Considering how dependent each of our daily decisions is on the accuracy of our assumptions, it's surprising we don't explicitly call out the suppositions we're making in a given situation. While assumptions are disparaged by most people, the problem is not making assumptions; it's *failing to recognize we're making assumptions*. This is problematic because it blinds us to evidence that our assumptions could be wrong. Just as the first step in solving an algebra problem is identifying the variables in the equation, identifying our assumptions up front lays the foundation for solving our problems accurately.

> *The problem is not making assumptions; it's failing to recognize we're making assumptions.*

When you're about to make a strategic decision for your team, for instance, put your assumptions on paper. Perhaps you're assuming your company's strategy will stay the same for the next three years, that your customers' needs will remain constant, or that your resources are limited to a certain dollar amount. Laying out these assumptions will force you to identify these beliefs, and it also opens the door for others to challenge their accuracy.

This process can also enable you to establish *tripwires* for your decisions. Coined by Chip and Dan Heath in their book *Decisive*, tripwires are conditions that prompt you to stop and reevaluate your course of action. When the executive team issues a new strategic plan, for instance, that action should prompt a new assessment of your decision because one of your core assumptions (i.e., that the strategic plan will remain constant for three years) was violated. As the leader, you can then reconvene your team and reexamine your plans. "When we made this decision six months ago, we assumed our strategic plan would not change. Now that our CEO has announced our new direction, let's revisit our plans to see if we're still in alignment." At worst, you spend a half hour revisiting a decision that still stands and you walk away with renewed confidence in your course of action. At best, your thoughtful pause helps you and others avoid wasting time and resources on an outdated direction.

If you dislike the thought of passively waiting to see if your assumptions will be proven false, you can go one step further and conduct experiments to proactively test your assumptions. Good entrepreneurs do this intuitively as they build a product or service they think customers need and refine it multiple times as they observe what customers like and don't like about their offering. But leaders entrenched in organizations generally fail to operate with this same entrepreneurial mindset about their choices, which is ironic considering they often have much more invested in the successful outcome.

For instance, if you think your organization needs a development program for high-potential leaders, your first step is not to write a proposal for a yearlong cohort with a five-figure price tag. It's to plan a book discussion group over the lunch hour and see who shows up, or to convince three established leaders to volunteer a few hours in mentoring younger professionals. Not only does testing your assumptions help you pinpoint the real problem you're trying to solve, but it also builds a business case for that full-fledged program down the road.

This process of stating and testing assumptions isn't just important for strategic decisions, though; it's also valuable in our relationships. As comedies demonstrate time and again, our relationships are plagued by mistaken assumptions. If left uncorrected, those false beliefs can poison our relationships.

Brené Brown, a research professor at the University of Houston, combats this problem with an artful phrase. When a friend or coworker does something that irritates, angers, or disappoints her, she reveals her internal narrative to the other person so they can correct it. Rather than accusing them of malicious intent, she transparently communicates her assumptions by saying, "The story I'm telling myself is…".

I used this framing recently with a friend after he cancelled a commitment with me at the last minute. Since I felt disappointment and resentment starting to build up between us, I addressed it directly with him. When we got together next, I said, "The story I'm telling myself is that you cancelled because our time together is not important to you. Knowing you though, I'm guessing that's not true. What really happened?" It turned out his boss scheduled a last-minute meeting with him, and he was just as frustrated by the change of plans as I was. We then had a productive conversation about how we can better coordinate schedules in the future to reduce frustration for both of us.

By identifying the narrative occurring in our own heads, we bring our reality into the light to examine whether it's true or not. We engage in healthy conflict with the other person by addressing hurt or disappointment, but we do it from a place of assuming our narrative could be wrong. When we share those perceptions with others, we honor them with the opportunity to clarify their intentions and correct any misunderstandings.

Whether in life or in leadership, calling out your assumptions leads to increased clarity and better decisions. Choosing to say, "Here's what I'm assuming. I might be wrong," is itself a great act of humility that often spreads contagiously to others as well.

Look "out the window" and "into the mirror"

One of the many memorable lines of *Good to Great* was Collins' description of how his Level 5 leaders handled both success and failure. When the organization accomplished a major goal, they looked "out the window" to find others who could be celebrated for their achievements. In contrast, when the company made a major mistake, they began by looking "into the mirror" to assess where they were personally responsible.

> *When we share those perceptions with others, we honor them with the opportunity to clarify their intentions and correct any misunderstandings.*

Most of us get this process reversed. In true Fundamental Attribution Error fashion, we give ourselves the benefit of the doubt while quickly casting blame on others. My Saturday chore story is a perfect example. That's why establishing a process for how to engage with success or failure can be so helpful.

The arrival of good or bad news should trigger us to focus attention on the right area first. If it's good news, look out to see who you can thank or celebrate for their genuine contributions. And if it's bad news, begin by taking responsibility for your part in the fiasco. Doing so is humbling: it increases your self-awareness while simultaneously elevating your appreciation for others' contributions.

To be clear, I'm not suggesting leaders should accept all blame and reject all praise. Taken to the extreme, such a practice would be theatrical and detached from reality. But if we choose to compensate for our natural self-protective biases by overcorrecting in this direction, we'll often find the people around us start to do the same. They'll stop playing the blame game and start to take more responsibility for their choices while cultivating an attitude of gratitude as well.

Regardless of how they choose to respond, your decision has consequences for your own character development. By being the first one to shoulder blame, you compensate for your self-protective biases and cultivate a more accurate self-perception. And by looking to share credit with others, you also humble yourself by appreciating others' contributions.

Study cognitive biases

The thumbnail sketch of cognitive biases in this chapter is just the tip of the iceberg, and learning more about these tendencies can be incredibly humbling. As Nobel laureate Daniel Kahneman states, we have an "almost unlimited ability to ignore our ignorance," and understanding the depths of your ignorance is a freeing exercise.

An entertaining introduction to our error-prone tendencies is *Being Wrong*. Written by journalist Kathryn Schulz, the book delves into the perils and joys of mistakes. *Decisive* by Chip and Dan Heath attacks the issue of decision-making specifically, providing multiple processes or frameworks for making sounder choices. And if you really want to challenge your assumptions about your own thinking, *Thinking, Fast and Slow* by Daniel Kahneman, *The Black Swan* by Nassim Taleb, and *The Signal and the Noise* by Nate Silver all provide deep reflection and enlightening research on this topic. Each of these books will help you enhance the accuracy of your self-perception and increase your humility.

Practice Restoration Therapy

One of the most powerful discoveries in my leadership and my marriage has been Restoration Therapy (RT), an approach to emotional and behavioral regulation that heightens both your awareness of your own thinking and your control over your response. Developed by Terry Hargrave (a psychologist) and Franz Pfitzer (a therapist), RT builds on the success of cognitive behavioral therapy by taking things one step further to the level of behavior change. Although I'm certainly not a therapist, I've found the four stages of the process to be powerful for me. They are:

1. **Feelings.** What emotions am I experiencing?
2. **Tendencies.** How do I typically react in this situation?
3. **Truth.** What is the broader reality?
4. **Action.** What's my new path forward (that counteracts my unhealthy tendencies)?

Here's how I implement this personally:

Once I begin to notice I'm feeling irritable and being snippy with my wife, a thought occurs. *Something is off. It's time to walk through the four stages of Restoration Therapy.*

I stop what I'm doing and walk through the four stages out loud (more about that in a minute). Had I been aware of this process during my bathroom-cleaning debacle, it would have gone something like this:

Right now, I'm feeling resentful because I think I'm being controlled and micromanaged (feelings).

I know that when I feel this way, I tend to become passive-aggressive, bitter, and sulky (tendencies).

The broader truth is that I have total control over my time and can choose a different activity and attitude if I want to. I also know my wife loves me and values me, not just for the chores I complete (truth).

So instead of sulking, I'm going to choose a positive attitude and finish what I started (action).

This process has been lifechanging for me. Hearing myself say these things out loud shocks my system into recognizing the years-old pattern of behavior that I'm drifting into. Putting it into words gets it outside of my own head and prevents me from spinning the same thoughts around for hours or behaving in a way I'll later regret.

Most of the time, walking through the process once enables me to course-correct. But sometimes, I have to repeat the process a few times to recalibrate to my new reality. As Hargrave and Pfitzer argue, the process of verbalizing these thought patterns and practicing new behaviors begins to cement the new neural pathways needed for long-term behavioral and emotional change. Perhaps with enough practice I will eventually not need to stop and course-correct at all; I'll just become more adaptable and easygoing with my honey-do list. But in the meantime, this process of examining my thinking and refocusing my thoughts has proved powerful.

By consciously thinking about how our thought patterns and emotions shape our behavior, we become humbler. Doing so requires that we acknowledge our flawed thinking and skewed perspectives, increasing our self-awareness and opening us up more to learning and growing.

Humbler in Two Minutes

- **State your assumptions.** When you find yourself irritated with someone, pause and write out your assumptions about their motives.
- **Look "out the window" and "into the mirror."** Consider a recent accomplishment that you're proud of. Who could you thank for contributing to it?
- **Study cognitive biases.** Read a free book summary of one of the titles mentioned here at fourminute books.com.
- **Practice Restoration Therapy.** Run a recent conflict through the Feelings-Tendencies-Truth-Action framework to see what you learn about yourself.

Pillar #2:

Appreciate Others' Strengths and Contributions

10

Ask Open-Ended Questions

Perhaps the single greatest way to improve your leadership effectiveness and grow in humility at the same time is to ask more and better questions. Asking good questions and listening to others are by far the most common skills I see lacking with the leaders I coach even though great listening is essential for great leadership.

Why are asking and listening so critical? Listening does several things for both the asker and the responder. For the asker, listening provides new information that could be valuable for understanding complex issues. As described in Chapter 4, the discipline of "balanced processing"—soliciting viewpoints that contradict our own beliefs and assumptions so we can see all sides of an issue—leads to better decisions overall. Balanced processing doesn't happen unless someone asks questions and listens well.

For the asker, listening and learning also deepens humility. Opening myself up to new ideas and learning something in the process reminds me how little I know and how much I need others, prompting me to ask even more questions and learn even more in the future. In a sense, asking open-ended questions creates its own virtuous cycle of humility.

The impact on the person being asked is perhaps even more profound. As professors Niels Van Quaquebeke and Will Felps argue in their research on "respectful inquiry," asking questions creates three feelings within the other person:

1. Control
2. Competence
3. Connection

Why these three? Well, when leaders ask you an open-ended question, they release control of the conversation. You have the option to respond however you'd like, and that empowerment creates a sense of control. Second, being asked for your perspective conveys you are competent as well. Asking leading questions that only have one right answer conveys I know the answer and I'm not sure you do. On the other hand, a genuine open-ended question communicates you have something to offer. Finally, respectful inquiry creates a sense of connection. When a person genuinely wants to know your thoughts on a topic, you're likely to feel that person values you enough to solicit your ideas. These three impacts are powerful, even life-changing, when they occur.

Despite all the benefits of open-ended questions, leaders often fail to ask enough of them. Some leaders are simply unaware of how to do it because they've never seen it modeled for them. Others know it's important but are too impatient to make space for it. And some leaders are either too insecure to show their reliance on others or too overconfident to recognize their interdependence.

Humble leaders find ways to overcome these barriers. They practice forming good questions to make asking them more natural and automatic. They slow down to make space for dialogue, knowing it will save them time overall. And they choose to deal with their own insecurities and appreciate the contributions of others by being vulnerable enough to ask inviting questions.

Here are a few ways to create a genuine sense of control, competence, and connection with others.

Ask the right kinds of questions
When it comes to engaging others in meaningful conversation, all questions are not created equal. If worded incorrectly,

questions can feel like an interrogation and promote defensiveness even if your tone and intentions are correct.

To prevent this problem, avoid *leading* questions ("Have you thought about...?" or "Why don't you...?") and *close-ended* questions ("Can you do this by _____?" or "Do you want _____ or _____?"). Instead, ask questions that give the responder an opportunity to respond openly. If your question has "you" as the second word (as in "Can you...?", "Will you....?", "Have you...?"), odds are the question isn't open—it's just a suggestion with lipstick on.

Instead, try beginning with "What" and "How" to create more opportunity for creative responses. Here are a few examples:

Closed question	Open question
Why did you do that?	What factors did you consider?
Do you think she's mad?	How might she be viewing the situation?
Have you tried writing things down?	What might be holding you back from being effective?
Could you talk to him?	How could you approach this situation differently?

Lastly, avoid "Why" questions. Why? Because getting asked "Why?" subconsciously puts you on the defensive. Imagine that you and a friend are walking to a meeting when a mutual friend stops you and tells you a lewd joke. Afterward, your friend asks you, "Why did you laugh at that joke?" What is your initial internal response to that question?

If you're like me, a range of emotions from shame to embarrassment to self-righteousness sprint through your body. Then comes the self-justification. *What was wrong with that joke? Didn't I see you smiling too? I was just trying to be polite; I didn't want to embarrass him.* Their question may have been free of judgment, but the response from you is testy and defensive.

If they asked instead, "How were you feeling when he told that joke?" you'll probably respond differently. You may still be defensive, but you're more likely to isolate the variables in your thought process than grasp for a narrative that vindicates your reaction. If you can reframe "Why" questions into "What" or "How" questions, you'll get closer to the answers you really want, and you'll draw out the unique perspectives of others.

Lightbulbs, not headlights

Have you ever had one of those "deer in the headlights" moments where someone said something that stunned you and left you speechless? One of my friends, a warm and outgoing Hoosier who was living in Boston, received one of these messages from a bristly New England acquaintance. "Your friendliness comes across as fake. No one's nice to everyone like that. I think you'll fit better back in Indiana."

In these situations, most of us would respond by either crumbling under the weight of their critique or becoming defensive and pushing back. No one likes that feeling. Ironically, though, our own well-intentioned efforts to be helpful often create the same result in others. So what's the alternative?

The best leaders "lead *to* insights, not *with* insights" as my colleagues at DDI say. When they do, they create "lightbulb" moments for others instead of the "deer in the headlight" responses: The

> *Lead* to *insights, not* with *insights.*

illumination comes from the inside out rather than outside in. People feel more empowered (since they're the ones coming up with the insight) and they are more likely to accept the idea (after all, it was theirs!).

Our minds often respond to outside feedback in the same way our body fights off an infection. Just as a healthy immune system fights off any foreign viruses, so too our rational powers leap to our defenses to explain away external critique or suggestions. But once those ideas are coming from within, our ideological immune systems give our bodies a chance to assimilate them. When you ask questions that lead others to have their own *Eureka!* moments, the people you're engaging with stay more open to new thinking, accept the new insights more readily, and remain empowered throughout the process.

One practical way to do this is to turn 80% of your insights into questions. Rather than jumping into a conversation to offer your perspective, challenge yourself to ask an insightful question that will get others thinking instead. If you can take four-fifths of your insights and reconfigure them into questions (i.e., "How would we know what the customer wants?" instead of, "The customer wants _____"), you'll find the level of thinking and engagement in your meetings skyrockets. Since humble leaders are always on the lookout for ways to draw out the best in people, this is a huge win.

Clarify and summarize

If someone says something you don't understand, ask for clarification. Don't pretend you get it if you don't. Clarifying questions show that you're listening and you care while also ensuring everyone stays on the same page. This latter outcome further increases the sense of connection that your conversational partner feels because you both stay more aligned during the discussion. So rather than rushing ahead to the end of the meeting, take a moment to slow down and clarify everyone's thinking.

Like clarifying, summarizing is a powerful way to ensure you and everyone else remain aligned. Saying, "If I'm understanding you correctly, you think _____" conveys you are listening, keeps the conversation on track, and brings additional clarity. While this step may feel like an unnecessary slowdown to the conversation, the impact is powerful.

A summarization can produce one of three outcomes, all of which are positive. If you correctly summarize what the person is thinking, you'll increase the sense of mutual connection in the conversation by showing them that you're listening closely. If you misunderstood what they said, your summary reveals the disconnect and enables you to realign your understanding to reality. And if you accurately summarize what they *said* but not what they *meant,* you'll help them understand themselves far better than they did before.

I observed this last phenomenon in a powerful way when coaching a friend. Steve had started a faith-based support group years ago, and now he wondered if it was time for him to step away and leave the operations of the group to others. After explaining his thought process for a while, I summarized what he said using a direct quote from him.

"So you think that if you leave the group, 'a lot of people will walk away from their faith?'" I asked.

"Yes," he agreed. He paused for a moment, then continued. "But you know, now that I hear my words said back to me, I don't think that's true. I mean, I *thought* it's true, but I don't think that's really accurate. And even if it was true, if I'm the only thing holding someone's religion together, that's a pretty dysfunctional situation."

That moment of insight provided valuable freedom for Steve, reducing some of the emotional pressure he felt when making his decision. The insight came not from a perspective I offered but simply from reflecting back what he was saying so he could see his own thinking accurately. I was humbled by the insight he produced on his own, too.

Humbler in Two Minutes

- **Ask the right kinds of questions.** Rewrite a closed question ("Could you...") as an open one ("How might you...").
- **Lightbulbs, not headlights.** Practice asking four questions before offering one observation.
- **Clarify and summarize.** Practice making every third statement a clarifying or summarizing one.

11

Listen Actively

If you're hunting for the fastest way to irritate another human being, the playbook is simple: just don't listen to them. Few things get our blood boiling like being ignored. If the insult doesn't lead to a fight in the moment, it will often seep down into the person and breed disengagement or resentment. As Andy Stanley says, "Leaders who refuse to listen will eventually be surrounded by people who have nothing significant to say."

Despite how self-evident this truth is, few of us are excellent listeners. We passively attend to what others say while our mind or eyes are roaming elsewhere. We fail to deeply attune to the needs of others because of boredom or distraction.

This is a problem that humble leaders must overcome. As the previous chapter explained, respectful inquiry communicates control, competence, and connection—but only if the question-asker stops to listen attentively. Without genuine listening on the other side, the interaction fizzles and the relationship can even be damaged.

> *Leaders who refuse to listen will eventually be surrounded by people who have nothing significant to say.*

But active listening is just as important for the leader themselves. By positioning our bodies and minds to give our full attention to others, we communicate engagement to them (by nodding, reacting, making eye contact, etc.) and we can understand them better. Deeply attuning to others enables us to take in more data (nonverbals, tone, and unspoken messages), and that rich data creates its own virtuous cycle of new insights, deeper connections, and better questions. After all, great questions come from great listening—meaning active listening is the foundation for any effective conversation.

Here are some practical ways to better practice active listening.

Stay curious

The biggest barrier to active listening is our own distractedness. We're not present in the moment because we're reliving an event from the past, worrying about something in the future, or jumping to conclusions based on what our conversation partner has already said. Regardless of what it is that's taking us out of the moment, the effect is the same: we're missing terabytes of data coming at us from the other person because our attention is focused inward, not outward.

One antidote to this problem is "staying curious," a concept popularized by author and executive coach Michael Bungay Stanier in *The Coaching Habit*. Staying curious means suspending judgment—turning off that voice inside your head that says, *That was a stupid decision*, or *What they need to do is…*. It means assuming you don't know the full story and you may not have the right answer—at least not until you've spent a long time hearing the other person's perspective. It looks like asking just one or two more questions than I typically would to unearth a bit more insight before offering my two cents.

One hack I use to quiet my internal narrative and become more present is scanning for more data. Prior to getting trained as a coach, I often found myself bored or distracted in conversations. But after hours of observing effective coaches in action, I realized they were guiding their clients to much greater insight than I was—in large part because they were picking up on much more data. It was like the difference between a toddler and a painter walking through an art gallery. We were both experiencing the same stimuli, but I was seeing mere colors and shapes while they were seeing nuanced works of art.

Once I became aware I was ignoring tons of data in my conversations with others, our discussions suddenly became more interesting to me. I started hunting for nuances and hidden messages. The mystery and richness brought the conversation alive to me, and the other person felt it, too. My questions became far more insightful and drew out much greater insight from the other person because now I was truly hearing what they were saying.

Now if I find myself drifting into my own head, I start to look for that extra data. Where does he hesitate? When does she become frustrated or excited? What ideas keep coming up? By looking for signals beyond mere words, my brain stays busier and I pay better attention. And by paying attention, I appreciate the contributions of others, draw out their best insights, and beat back the creeping fixed mindset in myself that says I should know it all if I'm going to be helpful.

W.A.I.T.

Some people need to be motivated with a proverbial kick in the pants to get moving. In my experience, however, top-performing leaders generally have the opposite problem. Much of their success has come from their bias for action and proactivity—meaning their biggest challenge is often knowing how and when to slow down. This is true in many areas of life, but especially with their words. Verbal restraint is thus essential for leaders trying to humbly listen well.

One of my favorite acronyms to help me practice restraint is WAIT. It stands for "Why Am I Talking?" When I first came across this acronym, it nailed me to the wall. I had been a coach and trainer for a year and a half, and I felt like my job was to talk. After all, if I was going to go hear someone speak, it's because I hoped they had something interesting to say. If I were hiring a coach, I'd want someone with pertinent expertise. Talking was the way coaches delivered value to the world. Or so I thought.

I now see things a bit differently. As a trainer and coach, my value is not in saying interesting things. Frankly, the internet is full of people who have more

> **W.A.I.T.:**
> **Why Am I Talking?**

pithy, exciting, or sensational one-liners than I do. My clients don't hire me to be impressed or entertained; they hire me because they want to change.

The distinction may seem small, but it's not. If I have to prove my worth by sharing expertise, you can bet I'm going to talk a lot—especially if I'm insecure. But if the way I help you is by helping you change, then I must choose my words much more carefully. A thoughtfully placed question could be dramatically more meaningful to you than my well-practiced speech about how to manage your priorities. A single, powerful idea is much more likely to drive you to action than a data dump of everything I know on the topic. By pausing to ask myself "Why am I talking?" I reorient myself to the larger goal. Is what I'm about to say going to help you move forward or not?

Ask yourself the same question. Will your comment or question move the group forward or derail it? Will it draw attention to you or elevate the thinking in the room? Ask yourself this question before opening your mouth, and you'll be amazed at the insight and restraint it provokes. Moreover, this grounding in your greater purpose helps you become humbler by meeting your conversation partner's needs rather than your own.

Count to three

Last is the important practice of giving others space to think. Can you imagine how much freedom you'd feel in a conversation with your boss if you knew the other person would never interrupt you? That you'd have all the space you needed to sort out your thoughts before they snatched control of the conversation away again? As unreal as this scenario may sound, this is an experience we can create for others on a daily basis.

I hate getting interrupted; for me, it often feels like a sign of disrespect. But to be honest, it's something I do far more often than I'd like to admit. Because of my zeal to offer an insight or ask a question, I rush in and prevent the other person from completing their thoughts or even changing their mind. At my worst, I create a conversational pace that breeds a scarcity mindset. You feel you've got to jump in with your thoughts now or you'll never have space to get them in later. And while that can be fun during friendly banter, it stifles the deeper thinking and connection that comes when you know my top priority is giving you space to think and speak from a place of peace.

Before you respond to what someone says, count to three in your head. It will feel like an eternity to you, but it gives your conversation partner a chance to breathe. They may even find they have more to say when they have a moment to stop talking and let their brain catch up with their mouth. If you can get comfortable with silence, you'll be surprised by what the other person fills it with. Again, you'll likely find that they had more insight than you thought they did, further increasing your appreciation for their strengths.

Humbler in Two Minutes

- **Stay curious.** Ask two more questions than you typically would, then offer your perspective.
- **W.A.I.T.** The next time you feel yourself getting emotional in a conversation, ask yourself, *Why Am I Talking?*
- **Count to three.** When someone is sharing something that is emotional for them and they pause, count to three in your head before responding to ensure they're finished.

12

Invite Others In

Perhaps you've heard the old one-liner, "Leadership would be easy if it weren't for the people." The joke would be funnier if it were less true. After all, leadership of any variety is intrinsically about people—influencing them, encouraging them, supporting them, aligning them. Even though we might prefer to swap out some of those people we are called to lead, we recognize that leadership and relationships are inseparable.

But while good relationships are important for any kind of leader, they are essential for humble leaders. Why? It's not because humble people are any more incapable or dependent than their self-absorbed counterparts. (As Chapter 3 showed, humble people can actually accomplish even more than their self-reliant peers.) Instead, humble leaders ardently pursue relationships because they more accurately recognize their need for them. They join peer groups and conduct self-evaluations not because they have more flaws but because they've come to terms with their flaws. They're not more limited, just more aware.

Why is inviting others in so important for humble leadership? As research shows—and as your parents probably told you—the nature and quality of your relationships exert tremendous influence over your life.

For instance, research finds that your college roommate has a direct impact on your GPA, attitudes toward race, likelihood to cheat, and dozens of other life choices. Those peer effects continue after college, with your immediate coworkers influencing your level of productivity, perseverance through difficult challenges, and even risk-taking behavior in office lotteries.

None of us is immune to these effects, including doctors. Their peer groups can influence them to work faster, order fewer tests, and spend less money on a patient's care, which may translate to worse results for their patients.

In short, the people we surround ourselves with have a dramatic impact on how we live and work. Leadership guru Jim Rohn goes so far as to argue, "You are the average of the five people you spend the most time with," meaning your peer group has a larger effect on your ongoing evolution than almost any other environmental factor in your life.

> *You are the average of the five people you spend the most time with.*

But even if you're not motivated by increasing your job performance or achieving that next career milestone, you should still take a close look at your relationships for one overarching reason: your own happiness. Researchers at Harvard who have been tracking the same cohort of men over the last 80 years came to these powerful yet simple conclusions about the importance of relationships:

> Close relationships, more than money or fame, are what keep people happy throughout their lives, the study revealed. Those ties protect people from life's discontents, help to delay mental and physical decline, and are better predictors of long and happy lives than social class, IQ, or even genes.

In short, close relationships serve as a ballast for weathering life's challenges.

Here are a few proven practices for inviting others in.

Slow down and consider your goal

Personally, my pace of life is the biggest barrier I face in developing close friendships or asking people to speak truth into my life. I have a strong bias for action that enables me to get a lot done, but that pace comes with collateral damage. Oftentimes in my haste to check something off the list I'll miss an obvious opportunity to solicit feedback from someone who could make my work significantly better. It's silly how hard it is for me to schedule a lunch, wait for feedback, or delay a deliverable so I can incorporate the feedback I heard. As much as I hate to admit it, I often confuse activity with productivity.

An alternative approach is stepping back to consider what my *real* goal is. If my objective is to write an email as quickly as possible so it's no longer on my to-do list, then it makes sense to fire it off after one read-through. But if my true goal is persuading someone to change their approach to a contentious issue, then completing the message quickly

> *Don't confuse activity with productivity.*

isn't the goal. It's effectiveness. That email must be powerful if it's going to shift someone's perspective. For it to be powerful, I need the refinement of others.

So slow down and ask yourself: What's my true goal? And based on that goal, what role do others need to play in my life? Answering these questions requires you to step back and consider your greater purpose. As you consider that purpose and assess your capabilities against it, this exercise in self-awareness will reveal how the gifted people around you can help you take a better next step.

Identify the right people (your "challenge network")

Once you've come to the realization that you need to be more intentional about your relationships, the question becomes *Who?* Of all the people you could pursue, who would most enrich your life?

Close relationships are important, but relationships with the right people are even better. As Collins said in *Good to Great,* "The old adage, 'People are your most important asset,' turns out to be wrong. People are *not* your most important asset. The *right* people are." Humble leaders have a sober enough understanding of their own limitations and high enough view of others' contributions that they devote significant energy toward surrounding themselves with the right people.

In *Think Again*, Adam Grant provides two broad categories of the people we need in our lives. The first is our *support network*: the cheerleaders and advocates who open doors for us and provide the encouragement we need to press on. The second is our *challenge network*: the skeptics who lovingly-but-honestly question our decisions to make us better. Together, these individuals provide the balance of challenge and support we need for leadership success.

While most of us naturally surround ourselves with the supportive type, few of us seek out challengers (or even know what to look for in one). Grant goes on to say that the best challengers have a healthy mix of *disagreeability*—they're not "yes-men"—and *good faith*, meaning they push back on you for your benefit, not due to their own insecurity or need to be right. They have what Kim Scott calls *radical candor*. They care for you personally while challenging you directly, as Brad the softball coach did for me.

> The best challengers have a healthy mix of disagreeability and good faith.

As you look for folks who fit both criteria, also think about which role *you* need to play in the lives of the people you're responsible to and for. Does your spouse need a challenger or a supporter? Better yet, *when* does your spouse need a challenger and when do they need a supporter? (Hint: Try asking them.) What about your boss, your direct reports, or your kids? As you intentionally craft these two networks for yourself, ensure you're also showing up the way you need to for the people who are most important to you. Doing so will foster more accurate self-perceptions, greater appreciation for others, faster personal growth, and better alignment to your greater purpose.

Build feedback mechanisms (the "daily review")

Cultivating the right relationships for feedback is essential, but the mechanisms for gathering insight are even more so. Why? Because even our trusted friends rarely offer unsolicited criticism. That's why great leaders go hunting for feedback and build systems to ensure they don't miss it at critical times.

One of the best feedback mechanisms I've come across is the "daily review" at Pixar. As documented in *The Pixar Story*, the acclaimed studio uses this process to rapidly gain honest feedback so individual contributors can quickly improve.

Every day at Pixar, animators walk into a theater full of award-winning storytellers, show the work they did the day before, and get feedback on it. Seasoned and novice creators alike are handed unvarnished insight that sparks innovative ideas, reveals blind spots, and prevents them from wasting time on unproductive paths. The result is not just stronger animation, but a growth mindset for the entire team.

Leaders at Pixar focus on learning from feedback not because it's fun, but because it works. By leveraging the collective insight of *all* their award-winning storytellers for a given project, they prevent animators from wasting their time and ensure the final product is fantastic, not just adequate.

As their record shows, the process works. Since first releasing *Toy Story* in 1995, the animation studio has earned 11 Academy Awards and over $14 billion at the box office for an average haul of $680 million per film. Sustaining quality results at this level over multiple decades requires more than just talented illustrators or compelling marketing campaigns; it requires effective feedback mechanisms.

Daily reviews are just one way to collect feedback, of course, and most of our work won't easily lend itself to this kind of cadence. Even still, as we think about how to develop the feedback mechanisms we need to become humbler leaders, analyzing what makes the daily review helpful can spark insight for how we could also replicate their secret sauce. Whether you are instituting a process as formal as a 360-degree review or something as informal as asking a friend for their thoughts, consider these six critical elements of the daily review:

1. **Immediacy.** Since feedback occurs immediately after their performance, there's less room for memories to get distorted in retrospect. *How can you collect feedback while it's fresh?*

2. **Short review cycle.** Because animators get feedback every day, at most they waste one workday going in the wrong direction. *How can you collect feedback early and often to avoid wasting time?*

3. **Automation.** Animators at Pixar don't have to wait until an annual performance review to know how they're doing, and they don't have to seek it out themselves: it comes every day whether they're ready or not. *How can you build systems or processes that will predictably give you feedback?*

4. **Negativity bias.** In contrast to how a bad restaurant manager asks for feedback ("Is everything tasting wonderful?"), the daily review is designed to flush out what's not working. *How can you make it safe and easy for people to share negative news?*

5. **Concreteness.** By giving feedback on specific work rather than an individual's general ability, the individual receiving feedback can focus on what they can change (the work) instead of being demoralized about what they can't quickly change (their ability). *How can you focus feedback on tangible, improvable areas of your performance?*

6. **Shared goal.** Some of the most trustworthy criticism comes from people who are pursuing the same goal with you, not critics from the cheap seats. *Who else has a personal stake in your success and wants to see you improve?*

Regardless of what you're soliciting feedback for, these elements can make your feedback gathering even more useful for your growth. Remember, wanting feedback and collecting feedback are two different things. If you genuinely want insight from others, you need to build a process to gather it. As best-selling author James Clear says, "We don't rise to the level of our goals; we fall to the level of our systems." We can't rely on hope or good intentions alone to drive change. We need a plan.

If you want to appreciate the insights of others and cultivate a growth mindset in yourself, building a mechanism for feedback is one of the best ways to do both.

Establish rhythms of accountability

If you are sincerely committed to personal transformation, one of the most potent wakeup calls is a rhythm of accountability. This looks like regularly (weekly or daily) connecting with a peer who will ask you tough questions that you have committed to answering honestly. During these sessions, you reflect with the other person on where you succeeded and where you failed, and you also take time to celebrate the wins and learn from the losses together. It's a space that's free from shame but radically committed to honesty and progress. Consequently, it deepens your self-awareness, makes you reliant on the support of another person, systematizes the growth mindset, and reconnects you to your larger purpose.

This process not only calls your mistakes out into broad daylight, it prevents you from making many of them in the first place. That's because once you have this rhythm established and you're honestly engaging in it, you start to anticipate the consequences of your choices in advance. When I'm at a crossroads, the question *Is this something I want to admit to Nathan when we talk on Monday?* sobers my judgment and helps me manage my worst tendencies more effectively.

I hesitated to include this action item because it sounds so strange and intense. Even still, I'd implore you to do it for the simple fact that it works. If you are serious about maturing or breaking the power of the past in your life, you need a healthy accountability relationship.

But you knew that already. You know the only reason you stuck to that one workout group for so long is you didn't want to disappoint the friends who were on the journey with you.

You've hopefully experienced the power of two people working together to achieve a goal that is personally relevant to each of you. It works not because your friends judge or shame you when you fail (if they do, it's counterproductive and breaks down the relationship), but because human beings intrinsically value keeping their commitments to other people. Despite our fantasies of being truly self-sufficient and independent, most of us care deeply about being people of integrity who do what we said we would do.

So where do you start? Well, if you've successfully slowed down to consider your goal and identify the right people, you know what issues you need to work on and with whom you should be working on them. The next step is the toughest: beginning to deepen your relationship with that person in the pursuit of greater transparency and commitment.

Honestly, it can feel a little like asking someone out on a date: you're vulnerably asking for a commitment you're not sure the other person will reciprocate. And then just as with dating, you take your time getting to know the other person through deepening conversations and shared life experiences, sharing small pieces of yourself at a time to ensure they will keep your confidence and remain judgment-free.

After years of slowly getting to know my friend Nathan, we began meeting on Monday mornings at 5:30 for accountability. During that time, we process the decisions we are wrestling with, confess our shortcomings over the last week, and hold each other accountable to our mutual commitments.

The practice was helpful from the start, but it hit a whole new level six weeks in. That morning, I'd just finished owning up to the failures that were top of mind for me—irritability toward my kids and overindulging my sweet tooth throughout the week. As I was wrapping up, Nathan asked, "Can I add another one to that list?"

My eyebrows shot up in surprise. "Yes, please!" I said, curious to hear what was on his mind.

"Well, I wouldn't be bringing it up except that it seems to be a pattern," he began. "On Tuesday night at dinner, Jack was running out into the street, and you made a comment toward Emily about how those things don't happen when you're watching him. You said it as a joke, but I saw the look on Emily's face, and it seemed like it hurt her."

I nodded. "Yeah, you're totally right. I absolutely threw her under the bus. That was wrong of me." He nodded in return.

"I'm not sure why I did that…" I said, pondering the situation. "Maybe it's because I feel a bit defensive about my parenting. Emily is always asking me to watch the kids more closely, and sometimes I feel she doesn't trust me. So when bad things happen on her watch, it makes me feel a bit more justified. I guess reminding her that she's not perfect was my way of justifying myself, but really I was just pulling her down to make myself feel better."

He nodded again.

"Thanks so much," I said, genuinely relieved. "I really appreciate you raising that to my attention. I don't want our marriage to be one where we drag each other down."

"For sure," he said.

"The one thing I'd ask in the future is that you don't wait until it's 'a pattern'," I continued. "Please know that one time is enough. If you see it, I want to know."

"You've got it," he agreed with a smile.

I left that conversation feeling more energized than I had in months. Nathan's radical candor communicated such care for me. He was attentive enough to notice the issue, and then lovingly confronted me about it. His willingness to make himself uncomfortable to help me get better conveyed volumes about our friendship. The interaction left me invigorated because I knew someone was in my corner and was watching out for my blind spots.

These accountability relationships are so life-giving, but they do require a lot of work. Accountability is far more than spilling your guts without wisdom to people you barely know. Getting to these levels of depth requires vulnerability, persistence, proactivity, and discernment. Choosing the right person is critical, too. Finding someone who will keep your confidence and not judge you feels like a tall order for many of us, which is why most of the people I know don't even begin searching.

The only shortcut I've found to this process so far is working with an executive coach. When I first started getting coached myself, I was amazed it only took a few sessions to create the depth of connection that often took months or years with other people. It makes sense, though. After all, a coach is trained to ask insightful questions and listen to you without judgment. Without this authentic connection, coaching relationships can't make much progress.

The other advantage coaching relationships carry is a predictable cadence. Meeting biweekly ensures participants don't go too long between conversations, encouraging them to stick to their commitments in anticipation. When I ask my coaching clients what helped them grow so rapidly or achieve so many of their goals, it's the accountability that surfaces most often as the key factor. Even though they are the ones with true power in the situation (i.e., they could fire me at any time), they still find the accountability I provide makes a real difference for their lives.

Regardless of whether you develop accountability relationships on your own or hire a coach or therapist to fill that niche for you, the result is powerful. When accountability takes place within the context of holistically strong relationships, you'll begin to see sustainable (and even fun) growth. Your mutual purpose of progress will unite you and spur you each on to action. Opening yourself up to hear truth from your partner affirms what they have to offer, sharpens your self-perception, and returns you back to the growth mindset again and again. When you walk together with people who are invested in your growth, you'll delight in the process of getting better, together.

Humbler in Two Minutes

- **Slow down and consider your goal.** Consider a project you've been working on for a long time. How does your stated goal compare to your actual effort?
- **Identify the right people (your "challenge network").** Jot down the names of three people who would be willing to give you tough feedback.
- **Build feedback mechanisms (the "daily review").** Brainstorm a few ways you could collect more regular feedback on your work and life.
- **Establish rhythms of accountability.** Schedule a walk with a friend to catch up on life and discuss some challenges you've been facing recently.

13

Solve Problems *with* People, Not *for* People

Many leaders I know wrestle with a terrible duality. Do they focus on results at the expense of relationships, or do they maximize relationships and sacrifice results? When faced with the choice between being loved or being respected, they often choose the approach that feels most comfortable for their personality and resign themselves to the consequences.

Humble leaders don't take this fool's bargain. They find ways to build strong relationships *and* deliver fantastic results. In fact, their results come *because* of their strong relationships, not despite them. However, getting things done through others requires these leaders to unlearn some beliefs they've internalized over the years.

One of those beliefs has to do with how they add value to an organization. In their early careers as individual contributors, they learned that their usefulness came from what they *contributed*. In contrast, a leader's value comes from *leading*. More specifically, success for a leader looks like creating *more value* through the people they lead. Consequently, leaders are no longer measured based on what they can get done *themselves* but what they can get done *through others*.

Unfortunately, many leaders fail to make this mental shift. They continue trying to add value to their teams by solving problems *for* people—thinking that keeping problems off their teams' plates is the best way to serve them. While their servant's heart is commendable and their choices are certainly right at times, the result is often that the leader gets overworked, the team members remain disempowered, and the solution that they provide is suboptimal because the leader was not the best person to solve the problem.

I once spent weeks building an Excel sheet for another department only to find out after dozens of hours of work that they didn't want it. I saw a problem and rushed into fix it without bringing others along, and the result was that my solution was dismissed in much the same way our bodies reject a foreign virus. Had I spent less time solving the problem *for* this team and more time solving the problem *with* the team, we might have come to an agreeable solution. Instead, the entire project was dead upon arrival, and the problem was never fixed.

This inclination to do things *for* others instead of *with* others is particularly tempting for men. As numerous research studies have documented, men overall are much more likely than women to prefer competitive environments rather than cooperative ones, and teams dominated by men tend to perform more poorly than those with a strong female presence.

Why the difference? Research by Peter Kuhn and Marie-Claire Villeval shows that men and women see themselves differently compared to their peers. Because women tend to undervalue their own abilities and highly esteem the contributions of others, they see the benefits of partnerships more clearly and are more likely to seek out collaborators. Once in those groups, the individuals with stronger interpersonal skills (who are more likely to be women) increase the performance of the group by listening better. Their effective interpersonal behaviors raise the intelligence level of their groups and confirm their initial hypotheses that they had much to gain from their colleagues, accelerating their virtuous cycle of humble leadership.

Here are a few things action items to help you begin that virtuous cycle of effective team dynamics for yourself.

Begin strategically

Before jumping into "doing" mode, assess yourself, your prospective partners, and the situation. *What do I have to offer uniquely within this situation? What can they bring? Whose expertise and perspective do we need to include in the process?* Thinking broadly will help you avoid the blinding influence of do-it-all-yourself-ness.

If you're prone to leaping before you look in situations like this, a procedural checklist can be helpful. Make a list of everyone you need to consult before making a certain type of decision or beginning a new project. This checklist will pull you up to the 20,000-foot view and help you make choices more in line with your greater purpose.

Seek first to understand, then to be understood

It's easy to assume everyone is either motivated by all the same things you are or isn't motivated by the right things at all. The truth is most of your collaborators will have different motivations simply based on their different vantage points, backgrounds, departmental goals, and resource constraints. And thank goodness for that! Without this healthy diversity of goals, your organization would err too far in one direction. If no one in your organization was motivated to control costs, for instance, it'd be easy for your visionary leaders to spend your organization straight to insolvency.

Even if your collaborators' goals are misaligned with the organization's priorities, it's important to recognize that their goals are just as valid to them as yours are to you. Everyone's goals, decisions, and motivations are logical in their own minds regardless of how illogical they may appear to you.

> *Everyone's goals, decisions, and motivations are logical in their own minds regardless of how illogical they may appear to you.*

So rather than jumping into the plan, make space to understand what's motivating your partners and how this process can produce a creative win-win for them. If you can begin by asking yourself the question, "What's in it for them?" you'll be much more attuned to your partners' fears and motivations. When you "seek first to understand" as the legendary

Stephen R. Covey says, you'll lay a much stronger foundation for future influence.

This process of slowing down to align goals touches all four pillars of humble leadership. By reminding yourself that your perspective is not the only valid one, you foster a more accurate self-perception. Choosing to listen to the perspectives of others intrinsically shows that they have something valuable to offer, too. Finally, keeping your ears open for new insights fuels a growth mindset and keeps you from straying from your greater purpose of collaborating effectively with your partners.

Frame the problem rather than outlining the solution

Once you have a good grasp on your partners' motivators and values, connect the dots between the problem or opportunity you see and what they care about. Don't assume they will be instantly motivated to drop what they're doing to work on your project. Instead, begin by shining a spotlight on the pain this problem is causing or the opportunity that is being missed.

If you lead with a solution, people will often spend their creative energy explaining why it won't work. But if you lead with a puzzle, they'll instead use their analytical abilities to think through a solution with you. In the process, you convert a potential critic to an invaluable ally by focusing on your mutual greater purpose, not your conflicting views.

Humbler in Two Minutes

- **Begin strategically.** Make a checklist of people to consult for the projects you commonly get involved in.
- **Seek first to understand, then to be understood.** Before your next meeting, write down your understanding of the other person's motives.
- **Frame the problem rather than outlining the solution.** Make a list of how this problem is affecting the other person, their team, and the organization.

14

Become a Multiplier

In Liz Wiseman and Greg McKeown's bestselling book *Multipliers*, the authors provide a data-driven case for a new kind of leadership—one that maps closely to this idea of humble leadership.

Their study contrasted leaders they described as *Diminishers* with those they labeled *Multipliers*. Diminishers saw themselves as *geniuses*, retaining decision-making power for themselves, hoarding resources for their own gain, and micromanaging their direct reports. Multipliers, on the other hand, were *genius makers,* drawing out the best in others through rigorous debate, empowering people with autonomy, and challenging others to do their best work. Multipliers got up to *twice* the quality and quantity of work out of their direct reports while increasing the team's engagement and morale.

The same year *Multipliers* was released, a groundbreaking study appeared in one of the world's leading academic journals, *Science,* that reinforced many of these ideas. Anita Williams Woolley and her colleagues decided to test a few fascinating hypotheses about group intelligence. First, they wanted to know if teams had their own intelligence quotient that was stable across situations. That is, are "smart teams" smart regardless of the kinds of challenges they face, or does their performance depend on the task? Second, what factors might predict group IQ? Is a team's intelligence driven by the smartest person in the group (the Genius Hypothesis) or by the average intelligence of the group members (the Weakest Link Theory)? Since smarter teams make better decisions, understanding how to boost performance here would be an invaluable asset for leaders.

Woolley's team conducted lab experiments to answer these two questions and found that teams did indeed have a stable IQ just like individuals do. Hypothesis #1 was confirmed.

But the most fascinating discovery was that the best predictor of a team's performance wasn't the average intelligence quotient of the group's members or how smart the most intelligent member was. Instead, it was the average *social* intelligence of the group. Their studies found that teams with high emotional intelligence engaged in more balanced discussions and consequently made better decisions. The group's ability to engage everyone's individual talent was what made the difference, not raw intellectual horsepower. In other words, it wasn't the star violinist who created a great orchestra. The best music came from groups with a strong conductor and healthy group dynamics.

Multipliers understand this intuitively. As my friend and Multiplier Davin Salvagno would say, they choose to "*be* the spotlight" rather than "being *in* the spotlight." Instead of hogging the stage in the client presentation or taking up disproportionate airtime in their weekly meetings, they use their influence to shine attention on others, drawing out all the good things they have to offer. This approach to leadership doubles down on the second aspect of humble leadership—appreciating others' strengths—and consequently gets the best out of their collaborators.

Here are a few ways you can become a multiplier.

Act like a talent scout

In one way, Multipliers function like archvillains in a comic book: they study the superpowers of the heroes in the story so they can exploit them. But unlike Lex Luthor or the Red Skull, they don't scrutinize their foes to uncover their weaknesses; they hunt for each person's unique abilities so they can deploy them more effectively. They intuitively understand that everyone has something powerful to offer the world, but most of those gifts will never see daylight unless they are intentionally unearthed. Consequently, they are on a constant mission to uncover the hidden abilities that exist all around them.

Tools like personality or strengths assessments can be helpful here, as they offer language for the unique abilities that others possess and remind us of our own gaps we need to rely on others to fill. But terminology alone is not enough. It's the talent scout mindset that differentiates Multipliers from the rest of us. They are hunters who are always surveying the terrain for the next opportunity.

One barrier to overcome here is our own lack of creativity. Once we think of someone in a certain role or context, it's hard to reimagine how they might be more effective in another setting. The problem with this limited thinking is that we all have talent; sometimes it's just terribly misapplied.

Imagine you had never seen or heard of a walrus, for instance. Then one day you're walking through your neighborhood park and spy a massive, whiskered, blob of a creature perched on the tree branches above you.[3] After overcoming your initial shock and determining that the creature was not a supersized squirrel, you might conclude the animal was lazy, overweight, unmotivated. Its girth and seeming lack of agility certainly wouldn't make it a threat to you.

Days later, you stumble across the rescued walrus at your local zoo. There, you watch it glide underwater with remarkable fluidity and viciously fight other males contending for the same mate. Its blubber, which at first seemed to be a sign of sloth, now forms a protective shield against the icy water and the tusks of other walruses. The same traits that caused you to underestimate the creature in one habitat now form its advantage in another. You realize you tragically underestimated the animal's capacity because you judged based on its performance

---

[3] It would have to be a BIG tree, as the average walrus weighs about 2,200 pounds.

in its setting at that moment, not its innate potential for success in a different environment.

So how can you avoid falling prey to this same "walrus-in-a-tree" blind spot? Here's one suggestion. The next time you have a chance to observe one of your coworkers or team members in action, ask yourself (or the other person) a few questions:

- What is it this person does naturally and consistently? (Traits that annoy you may quickly stand out here.)
- What do they enjoy most about their jobs? Least? (Where does their energy naturally flow?)
- If I was building a position from scratch for them to take advantage of their natural inclinations, what kind of work would they do? (In other words, what's their natural habitat?)
- What kind of value would that work add to our organization? (How could they help our ecosystem flourish if their natural gifts were maximized?)

This kind of blue-sky thinking helps you break free of the anchoring biases that someone's current position may create for you. By starting with a clean slate, you can now imagine new ways of drawing out what they have to offer.

Perhaps you have the power to redefine the role yourself and make it happen. If so, consider it. But odds are you can't wave a magic wand today. Instead, try tailoring the work you send their direction to match their skills and passions. And when you see their strengths in action, celebrate it.

Express appreciation for others

Adopting the talent scout mindset helps you deepen your own appreciation for others' contributions, but cementing that outlook in your own mind and in the minds of others requires that you get those thoughts out of your head. As described in the section on Restoration Therapy, saying things out loud makes the ideas more concrete and memorable for ourselves—but the impact those thoughts have on the people we're trying to lead humbly is even more profound.

Can you think back to a proclamation a teacher or mentor made about you in your formative years? Perhaps they told you that you were a leader or you had talent. Maybe they said you'd never amount to much or you couldn't get into that university.[4] Whether the message was positive or negative, you know intuitively how powerful words are. As Rabbi Abraham Joshua Heschel says, "Words create worlds," even if those words are untrue.

As leaders striving to become humbler and draw out the best in others, we have the chance to harness the power of words for the good of others and create worlds in which they see the true extent of their potential. Doing so requires that we go beyond thinking positive thoughts about others and take time to express them.

Take time to write a note, send an email, or give a literal pat on the back to someone. When you're prompted to thank someone for their contributions, follow the advice of HP cofounder Bill Hewlett: "Never stifle a generous impulse." Act on that impulse to be grateful, and you'll find that the engagement and joy of your team increases. Pass up that opportunity, and you may learn the hard way that "Unexpressed gratitude is experienced as ingratitude," as Andy Stanley says. Don't assume your friends and colleagues understand the depth of your appreciation for them; eliminate all doubt by stating it repeatedly. In doing so, you'll also strengthen your appreciation muscle for future use.

Follow your followers

One of the best ways we can demonstrate humble leadership (while also boosting the talent around us) is by following our

---

[4] Michelle Obama's high school guidance counselor famously told her she'd never get into Princeton—which she did, before getting into Harvard Law.

followers. By elevating the people we are responsible for into leadership roles, we model the growth mindset and appreciation for others that are essential for humility, and we stretch (and often humble) them, too.

I can think of one substantive time my parents hit this out of the park, and it changed me as a leader. My family runs a Christian campground outside of Waco, Texas, and every year, they and their staff orchestrate a few three-day summer camps for up to 100 local kids.

My junior year of college, my mom asked if I wanted to direct that year's camp. The offer gave me pause. I would be 20 years younger than any previous camp directors (most of whom had been my dad), and my parents would technically be reporting to me. To calm my hesitations, they let me know that they'd assist me in whatever ways they could and would not be fighting for control.

I said yes, and true to their word, they supported me brilliantly. When I set a direction, my mom implemented it eagerly. When problems arose with the campers, my dad brought them to my attention and asked me how I wanted to handle them. They offered counsel and perspective but restrained themselves from exerting control. We worked together as an effective team, and the result was a win for everyone.

Although I made some beneficial improvements as the camp director, I surely gained more from the experience than the campers did. Coordinating dozens of volunteers (all of whom were older than I) and facing unexpected challenges over an intense three-day period stretched me tremendously while increasing my confidence in my own leadership.

I also grew to appreciate what my parents and other camp directors had gone through to make camp worthwhile for the kids and volunteers. And most of all, my respect for my parents grew. Far from imbuing me with a sense of superiority over them, I was humbled by their own act of humility and appreciated them even more for it.

When we choose to follow our people, we communicate confidence in them that words alone cannot convey. Saying that others have "leadership potential" is in many ways an empty affirmation that costs us nothing. But placing a project or event in their hands and choosing to *follow* them shows them you are willing to place a real bet on their abilities. And when that bet proves to be a winner, everyone benefits.

You are one of the individuals who benefits from that process, of course. As you choose to be led by someone else, you cast a vote for your greater purpose and tell your ego to take a backseat. You embody the growth mindset at an organizational level too, showing that you don't have to be seasoned or polished to take on new opportunities. Instead, you invest in the growth of the people around you to develop their unique strengths and contributions.

Humbler in Two Minutes

- **Act like a talent scout.** Consider the person who annoys you the most. What would their perfect job be?
- **Express appreciation for others.** Shoot a text to someone you are grateful for, noting one specific trait or behavior of theirs and the impact it has made on you.
- **Follow your followers.** Identify one task in which you could follow a peer/direct report/child.

Pillar #3:

Growth Mindset

15

Cultivate a Growth Mindset

As described in Chapter 2, individuals with a growth mindset believe their abilities are not anchored to their talent; they can change with effort. Furthermore, they see success in life as the natural outcome of a good process. Invest in the right process, and you'll grow while producing better outcomes at the same time.

To put it another way, leaders with a growth mindset share two elements: the right goal, and the right attribution. First, their goals are centered on things they can control: doing their best, getting better, or giving maximum effort. A growth-minded person who is practicing shooting free throws, for instance, would focus more on the number of shots they take every day than the number they miss. Second, they appropriately attribute success and failure to things they can control as well: their effort, strategy, or process. Our free-throw shooter doesn't blame the ball or the basket for a missed shot; they focus instead on their shooting motion. Doing so gives them agency in the process and control over their destiny.

Why do these two elements matter? Leaders whose goals are *performance-focused* ("I want to show I'm competent") compared to *growth-focused* ("I want to do my best") will show high motivation to perform but will also demonstrate greater fragility or helplessness when they don't achieve according to their own expectations. As one of my coaching clients put it, they become "anxious overachievers." Even when they do perform well, the result is often more anxiety, as they now worry about how much they need to produce in the future to continue to reach the higher bar they just set.

Similarly, individuals who don't have the right attribution give credit for success or failure to things they can't control, like external circumstances or their own talent level. In doing so, they subconsciously disempower themselves. After all, if you believe you failed because of a lack of talent, why would you be motivated to try again? And if you believe you succeeded because of your innate skill, what motivation would you have to work any harder?

> *Leaders with a growth mindset share two elements: the right goal, and the right attribution.*

Growth-minded leaders take a different approach. Instead of believing they failed a performance evaluation because "my boss was out to get me," they look back at their priorities, work quality, and decision-making processes to examine what they could have done differently. Their goal is not to shoulder all the blame for failure but to properly control the things they can realistically influence.

One other thing you should know about growth mindset: having it in one area of life does not mean it automatically spills over to others. For example, a few years into my obsession with growth mindset, my wife and I were having our 31st fight about how to load the dishwasher correctly. After being told yet again I was not stacking things correctly, I threw up my hands in disgust. "Fine!" I said. "You can just do all the dishes from now on."

As my senses returned a few minutes later, that internal voice inside my head started pestering me. *Really, Josh? You're not loading the dishwasher again? EVER? Y'all have been married for less than three years, and your goal is to make it 60 or more. You're telling me that for the next 57 years you are never again going to load the dishwasher?*

My annoying inner voice had a point; 60 years was a long time to enforce a dishwasher-loading embargo. But the voice wouldn't leave me alone there. *And what about the whole "growth mindset" thing? You're telling me you can push yourself to get a PhD but you're not smart enough to figure out how your wife wants the dishwasher loaded? Does growth mindset work or not?*

I've never wanted to punch an invisible voice so much in my life. Despite my annoyance, the voice was right. I was consciously choosing helplessness in the situation instead of working to get better, and that decision was inconsistent with the character I wanted to develop in myself. So for the sake of marital peace and my own growth as a person, I stopped sulking and learned how my wife wanted the dishwasher loaded. As I did, my Do-Become Flywheel turned a little faster.

If you're interested in deepening this mindset in yourself, what can you do? Here are a few practical ideas to that end.

Assess your goals (and set the right ones)

Look at the goals you've set (consciously or subconsciously) for yourself. Are they performance goals, or process goals? Or as Adam Grant puts it, are you in *proving mode* (trying to show your worth) or *improving mode* (doing whatever it takes to get better)? If the former, how can you shift your mindset to the latter?

> *Hitting a new performance high is an indicator that you're on the right path, not a sign that your journey has concluded.*

Don't get me wrong: you should measure performance. We wouldn't enjoy sports nearly as much if they didn't keep score, and telling your boss you no longer want to be assessed based on performance will likely lead to some awkward conversations for the two of you. Performance does matter, but it's better conceived of as a milestone than an end goal.

Hitting a new performance high doesn't give you permission to coast, for instance; it tells you that the work you're putting in is producing results. It's an indicator that you're on the right path, not a sign your journey has concluded. Hopefully, you will continue to get better at life and leadership until the day you die. Setting goals that have a continuous improvement

158

bent are thus much more likely to keep you engaged in your work even as you achieve some degree of mastery. For the free-throw shooter, this might look like shooting 1,000 shots a day and having the goal of improving the percentage made every week.

Remember, the goal is progress over perfection. Or as Grant says, "The best way to *prove* yourself is to show that you're willing to *improve* yourself." By focusing on imperfect progress, you cast another vote for the growth mindset within yourself and humbly open yourself up to getting better.

Control what you can control (and let go of everything else)

Now that you've set the right goal, it's time to attribute responsibility accurately. And since you won't always be able to control the outcome, holding yourself doggedly accountable for results will only lead to ulcers. If you don't believe me, just go to a middle-school football game and study any of the zealous parents in the stands. As you watch them shout, scream, and throw up their hands in disbelief, you'll be reminded that this is how it feels to be passionate about achieving a result and yet utterly incapable of controlling the outcome. Nobody wins in that scenario.

> *The goal is progress over perfection.*

Consequently, you want to hold yourself fiercely responsible for effort but only loosely accountable for results. You have influence over outcomes, not control over them. When you conduct your post-mortem of the event, objectively analyze what you could have controlled and what you couldn't.

This means that neither a good outcome nor a bad one determines success or failure on its own. A thorough analysis of your process may reveal, for instance, that your good results came from luck, not your halfhearted effort. Similarly, even a perfect process can fail if events outside your control occurred. By taking an unbiased and open-minded approach to reviewing

159

your process and outcome, you'll ensure you control the one thing you can always control: your learning.

When I've shared this idea with leaders, a few have resisted. "I want my people to be accountable for results, though," they've said. "I don't just want them to throw up their hands and say, 'Well, I tried.' If they're not hitting their numbers, I want to see them innovating, questioning their process, and pushing themselves harder. I don't want to create room for excuses. And besides, if they're not producing results, they may lose their job, even if they're trying hard."

This is an understandable perspective, and these leaders are right about at least one thing: making excuses and choosing passivity will kill your team's culture and productivity. But when properly applied, "controlling what you can control" doesn't leave room for excuses. In fact, it increases accountability by forcing you to ask tough questions. Did I really give every ounce of effort possible? Did I follow the best process? Was I as prepared as I could have been?

Answering these questions honestly almost always reveals room for growth, improvement, and innovation. Rather than limiting our accountability, it enhances it by focusing it on the areas in which we have agency.

Measure (and celebrate) progress

To maintain your momentum for the long haul, you'll want to find ways to measure and celebrate the small wins you're accruing over time. Doing so reminds you at a cognitive level that what you're doing is worth the sacrifice. These rewards also work on a physical level, strengthening the neurological connections needed to make the behavior habitual.

This is again where performance measures can be useful. Whether you choose to record that progress in a dashboard, journal, scoreboard, or some other means, make time to create some sort of chronicle of your journey. And when you achieve a milestone, make space to celebrate it.

Many of the leaders I coach like celebrating others but can't bring themselves to celebrate their own successes. "It's like I'm afraid that if I stop and celebrate, all my drive to achieve again will go away," confessed one of my more self-aware clients. "What's made me successful is my constant drive to keep achieving, and I'm afraid of losing that momentum." Their fear of alleviating any performance tension consequently keeps them in perpetual motion, racking up achievements they never pause to enjoy. Worse still, they run the risk of underachieving over the long haul because further accomplishments cease to be motivating. After all, why would they continue pushing themselves to hit arbitrary goals if it's never fun for anyone?

To hack this same tendency in myself, I find it helpful to pre-plan some of these celebrations. Doing so ensures I follow through when the time comes. Anniversary trips, big parties on milestone birthdays, and congratulatory dinners are a few celebrations I've personally found meaningful in the past. Regardless of how you choose to celebrate, find a meaningful way to memorialize growth and remind yourself that you are a constant work in progress. Doing so reaffirms that growth mindset and makes your self-perception that much more accurate.

Seek out an opportunity to be a novice

Most people have no problem receiving feedback and adjusting our behavior when we're new to an activity. After all, we recognize intuitively that we have no clue what we're doing. We're hungry to learn in those early days because we want to get better, and we're generally easygoing when our performance stinks. It's to be expected, after all.

But then for some reason, a switch flips one day and our expectations for performance skyrocket. It's no longer acceptable to hit a golf ball into a sand trap; now you swear and throw a golf club into a pond. What changed?

My guess is that even though you appeared to be operating from a growth mindset early on, you weren't chasing the right goal. You wanted to learn, and you focused on improving the process, but your goal was the wrong one. Instead of focusing on continuous improvement, your implicit goal was to become

161

The Beginner's Fallacy

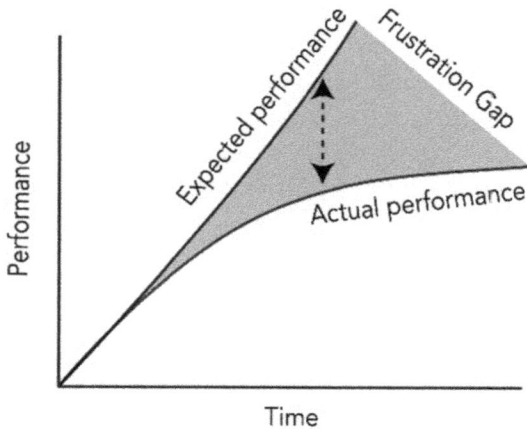

competent as quickly as possible. You were enjoying the learning process as long as growth was quick and measurable, but the second your performance plateaued or declined, your delight dissipated. And since growth comes most rapidly in the beginning, you either prematurely assumed you'd arrived or expected the growth trajectory to be linear instead of logarithmic. You fell prey to the Beginner's Fallacy.

So how can you use this experience to your advantage? Since it can be challenging to choose a growth mindset for something you already feel highly competent in, choose an activity where you are awful and commit to enjoying the learning process. By starting with a blank slate and "thinking about your thinking" (metacognition!), you can test out the growth mindset concepts in a low-risk environment. As you do, perhaps you'll find that this teachable spirit begins to show up in other parts of your life and leadership, making the growth mindset more pervasive for you in general.

Put yourself in the driver's seat

Feedback is a finicky thing for me. It's the most helpful thing in the world when I want it and need it. I am so grateful when someone gives me a nugget of wisdom after a presentation that helps make my work even better next time. But that same advice can feel like an attack if I wasn't expecting it—what leadership guru Joseph Grenny calls getting "feedsmacked."

When we are surprised by criticism, our egos often seize control of our physical responses and limit the amount of additional information. We stop hearing their critique out of self-defense, but that response also prevents us from stepping back to evaluate the person's perspective objectively to see if there's anything we can learn from it.

The solution to this dilemma is simple: just ask for feedback constantly. Ironically, the very act of inviting it makes it seem less offensive. After all, you *literally* asked for it.

I had to utilize this tactic myself when writing the book. After finishing the first draft of the manuscript, I was feeling good about what I'd accomplished. Several friends had read early revisions and provided largely positive responses, reinforcing my belief that I was on the right track. Then my friend and fellow consultant Mike sent over his three-page response. I saw his email come through while I was on the way to lunch with a friend, so I opened his notes up at a stoplight. "Starts to read like a personal account of becoming humble; paradoxically, it sounds like this is about you....This chapter is WAY too long....This is redundant." And so on.

I grimaced and sat my phone down as the light turned green. I could feel my face flushing as I drove, my body tightening, my mind racing to analyze and defend myself against his comments. I wanted my book to be great *already.* I was hoping for praise, not criticism. I was daunted by all the work I'd have to do to fix the issues he raised, so I wanted to find a way to explain away his perspective. As I rolled into the parking lot of the Vietnamese restaurant where I was eating that day, I closed my eyes and chanted to myself, *I asked for this. I asked for this. I asked for this.* Reminding myself I was the genesis for this feedback somehow made it more palatable. It reminded me that I sought it out so my book could get better. That perspective helped decrease my resistance and enabled me to find some gratitude amongst the pain.

It took a week for the sting to fully subside—though it got worse before it got better. I revisited the feedback a few hours later and felt my gut sink even further when I had the scariest thought yet: *He's right!*

For a few days, I was overwhelmed with what to do about this new reality. Lacking a plan for how to solve the problems he'd raised, the tension stayed in my body. But then one morning, I had a lightbulb moment and figured out how to reorganize my chapters to solve his issues. The energy I'd been exerting to resist and worry about this problem was now unleashed toward creatively solving it, and the writing flowed. My sadness turned into joy as I realized the book was now going to be much better after swallowing the tough medicine my friend had graciously given to me.

> *Bad leaders reject criticism, good leaders accept it when it comes, but great leaders go hunting for it.*

You too can benefit from the insights of others by putting yourself in the driver's seat. Asking for feedback consciously casts a vote for the growth mindset and reduces the resistance you naturally feel toward criticism. So give it a shot yourself. After all, bad leaders reject criticism, good leaders accept it when it comes, but great leaders go hunting for it.

Practice self-acceptance

For the high-performing leaders I work with, this last step—forgiving themselves for making mistakes—is perhaps the most challenging. For their entire lives, they've pushed themselves to be the valedictorians, team captains, and fast-tracked leaders. The inner critic is loud, always pointing out how they could have done better, spurring them on to work even harder next time.

The challenge is that while this inner critic raises the floor of expectations for these leaders, it also sets a low ceiling.

It pushes them to strive, but it cripples them with poisonous messages of inadequacy. While their fault-finding eye enables them to distinguish themselves by their excellence early in their careers, the hollow fear it leaves behind makes them vulnerable as life and career pressures increase. Left unaddressed, they become insecure, defensive, anxious, and burned out. As the famed executive coach Marshall Goldsmith memorably states, "What got you here won't get you there." Their exacting standards for themselves are now a liability, not an asset.

As a recovering perfectionist, I've seen the ravages of the inner critic firsthand. I was so hard on myself in high school that I would do pushups on the sidelines of football games to punish myself for throwing an interception. That drive enabled me to graduate at the top of my class, but it started to unravel in college. I entangled myself in an unhealthy romantic relationship and stuck with it despite counsel from plenty of friends that I was making a mistake. When the relationship imploded, as I knew it would, I spent two months beating myself up for it. *How could I be so stupid? Why didn't I listen? Can I not trust myself anymore?*

I was a basket case for weeks—randomly crying at unexplained times and lacking motivation to do more than the bare minimum. I had the same conversation in my head day after day, never making progress. At my lowest moment, I broke down crying on stage in front of all my friends while my band played on without me—tears and snot streaming unhindered onto my bass guitar.

It took an intervention from my parents and friends to snap me out of the cycle. As they prayed over me and demonstrated the kind of unconditional acceptance I so desperately needed, I finally realized that punishing myself for past mistakes was fruitless and frankly self-centered. If God had already forgiven me, I needed to learn from the mistake, let it go, and move on. That was a turning point in my relationship with perfectionism.

Like many of the high-achieving leaders I coach, I often need to cut myself some slack when I make mistakes. That's scary, though, because I fear that letting myself off the hook will lead to my downfall—as if accepting any imperfection in myself will lead to me morphing into a couch potato for eternity. In those moments, I have to remind myself that I am human, I will make mistakes, and the most productive thing I can do is learn from the situation and move on. Accepting myself is not defaulting to apathy but committing to reality.

Ironically, when you learn to forgive yourself, you'll find you can work harder because you're not wasting energy on self-flagellation. Instead, you focus on the things you can control and invest your time into productive changes. Amazingly, choosing forgiveness means becoming more relaxed and productive at the same time. And guess what? You also start being kinder and more gracious to all the other flawed human beings you interact with daily as you put the fixed mindset to death in another small way. It's a triple-win.

Humbler in Two Minutes

- **Assess your goals (and set the right ones).** Identify one area where you feel you have something to prove.
- **Control what you can control (and let go of everything else).** Reflect on a recurring source of frustration. What's something you're trying to control there that you can't?
- **Measure (and celebrate) progress.** Celebrate a milestone in a group text message with your friends.
- **Seek out an opportunity to be a novice.** Try a new sport or activity. Expect to be terrible.
- **Put yourself in the driver's seat.** Ask a coworker, "What's one thing I could do to be a better coworker?" and write down their answer.
- **Practice self-acceptance.** Identify one past mistake that you still haven't forgiven yourself for.

Pillar #4:

Greater Purpose

16

Discern Your Purpose

To stick it out with the challenging work of leading humbly, you've got to be committed to a purpose that makes the sacrifice worth it. As psychiatrist Victor Frankl found during his internment in a concentration camp (and subsequently chronicled in *Man's Search for Meaning*), "Life is never made unbearable by circumstances, but only by lack of meaning and purpose." A higher sense of purpose enables people to focus, persevere, and prevail even when the odds are stacked against them. Philosopher Friedrich Nietzsche poignantly captured this idea when he said, "He who has a 'why' to live can bear almost any 'how'." Clarifying your "why" thus enables you to make the difficult sacrifices needed in leadership.

A sense of purpose is necessary for all of us, but it's especially critical for humble leaders. Setting aside our own preferences to do what is best for our team or organization requires a commitment to a purpose outside of ourselves. If you don't care more about taking care of your customers than you care about remaining comfortable, you're probably not willing to have an awkward conversation with your underperforming peer. If you don't have a strong commitment to higher values like integrity and character, you're not going to work as hard at 4 pm on Friday as you did at 8 am on Monday. In short, living and leading with purpose requires that we pursue a purpose greater than ourselves.

> *"He who has a 'why' to live can bear almost any 'how'."*

All the humble leaders I know wage a daily battle to avoid settling for self-centered purposes like their own advancement, protection, or success. Instead, they remind themselves of the relationships they want to strengthen, the people they want to invest in, and the missions they hope to achieve.

Occasionally, leaders can crystallize their defining purpose into a single goal that defines an entire season of their lives. They find a cause outside of themselves in which they truly discover themselves. One of those leaders was Florence Nightingale.

Born into an affluent British family in 1820, Nightingale was classically educated, and her family expected her to marry and live a life of social ease. But in her late teens, she felt called by God to become a nurse—a totally undignified profession in Victorian England. Despite the protests of her family, she stubbornly pursued that vocation.

After war broke out between Russia and the British Empire on the Crimean Peninsula in 1853, Nightingale became aware of the dire need for nurses on the front lines. Again compelled by her greater purpose, she gathered a few dozen volunteers and sailed thousands of miles to Constantinople.

The situation she discovered upon arrival was dismal. Patients were laying in their own excrement; rodents and fleas were everywhere. Wounded soldiers were dying from infectious diseases before their war wounds could even be treated. In fact, the odds you would survive your wounds when you entered the hospital were little better than a coinflip—*40% of patients never walked out again.*

But Nightingale was undeterred. She organized patients to clean the place from floor to ceiling, established a laundry to reduce contamination, and started using her connections back in England to get the supplies they needed. And in a mere 18 months, she lowered the fatality rates from 40% to 2%.

Arriving back in England, she unexpectedly received a hero's welcome and a cash prize of 250,000 pounds from Queen Victoria, a sum that would be worth tens of millions today. Instead of keeping the money and retiring to a life of ease, she used it to start a hospital and nurse training school.

For the rest of her life, she worked tirelessly to improve medical care and sanitation everywhere. Despite contracting a disease on the war front that left her largely bedridden for the rest of her life, Nightingale continued to correspond with medical professionals all around the world and share her insights on medical sanitation.

When she passed away in 1910, King George V offered the family an elaborate state funeral and burial next to Charles Dickens, Charles Darwin, and Isaac Newton in Westminster Abbey. But in keeping with her humble wishes, her family declined the offer and interned her remains with family instead. From the earliest years of her adulthood until her death at the age of 90, Florence Nightingale was ceaselessly ambitious and relentless—but not for herself. Just like the Level 5 leaders that Collins profiled in *Good to Great,* she spent herself in service of something larger than herself.

While we may not all find a cause as grand as Nightingale's, living humbly requires us to dedicate ourselves to purposes beyond ourselves. But the question is: how do you know what that cause is? Whole books are written on this question, so what follows is necessarily incomplete. But in my process of discerning and refining my purpose and helping other leaders do the same, I've found that exploring these three elements of purpose to be a helpful starting place.

1. **Passions:** What you love.
2. **Strengths:** What you're good at.
3. **Flourishing:** What fosters peace.

At the intersection of these three areas is your purpose. Here's how to get greater clarity on each of those areas.

Reflect on your passions

One of the best ways of recognizing what you care about is to identify the things that raise your energy level—both in

The Three Dimensions of Purpose

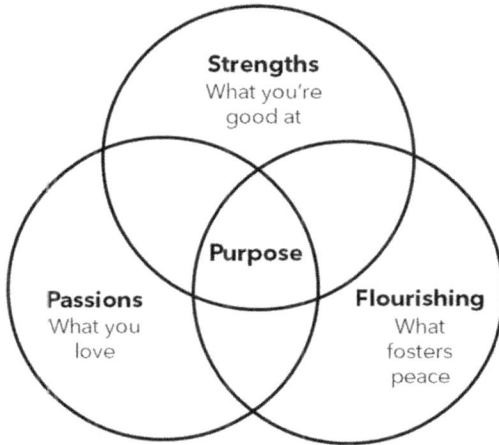

a positive and in a negative way. What do you get excited about, and what frustrates you or breaks your heart? Strong emotions on either side reveal that you care, and these are indicators of passion. Similarly, ask yourself, "What would I do for free? And what's the best hour of my week?" These questions can reveal the activities that generate the most energy for you and bring greater concreteness to the conceptual questions of passion.

This latter question was particularly powerful for me as I considered whether to stay in higher education or launch fully into leadership development. Thinking back over the best hour of my week, it was inevitably a time when I was coaching one of my direct reports I saw how the professional issues we worked on together also created breakthroughs in his personal life, and that holistic impact was invigorating. I had a passion for helping people live more meaningful lives, and something about working directly with people to help them achieve a breakthrough stirred my heart. When I realized I could spend

> *What's the best hour of my week?*

100% of my time rather than 1/40th doing that kind of work, the insight gave me the courage to leap out of the boat toward this new career.

As you reflect on your natural passions, you'll discern where your energy is naturally flowing. This self-insight will enable you to take the first big step toward discovering the greater purpose that will anchor your humble leadership.

Assess your strengths

Beyond what you enjoy doing, what are you good at? What do you get complimented on? What do you find easier to do than most people? These questions can be hard to answer on your own, as your strengths come so naturally to you that you may not recognize how unique they are.

Consequently, getting some outside perspective is crucial. Use an assessment like CliftonStrengths to understand your abilities at a generalizable level, then think through how those talents filter into how you do what you do. Ask questions of people who know you well, such as "What do you think my strengths are? What unique value do I add to the world?" Their answers will reveal not just what your strengths are but why they're so valuable.

During my first year of college, I had a lightbulb moment regarding my strengths that changed the course of my life. I was in class discussing the results of my CliftonStrengths assessment—specifically, my Strategic theme. As the professor was explaining the theme, it seemed like he was describing something that everyone did naturally, not a unique ability. I asked the class, "Doesn't everyone have a visual map of the campus in their heads where they see the most efficient path between any two buildings? Don't you all know which route to take to get from each building to the other as quickly as possible?" My classmates looked back at me like I was an alien. Apparently, I was an outlier here; I thought everyone thought that way. Becoming aware of this blind spot was itself illuminating and humbling.

I realized that while I was bad at many things, one thing I was good at was cutting through all the noise to identify what was really important. This realization later led me to ask, "If this Strategic ability is one of my unique talents, how can I leverage it to my advantage?" That question eventually led me down the path of strategically analyzing leaders and their organizations to help them map out a more effective path to meet their goals. A trait I once took for granted has now become a strategic advantage in my career.

Taking time to reflect on your own strengths will help you figure out not just what you care about, but where you can effectively make an impact. Combining your strengths and passions in this way creates powerful focus for your greater purpose.

Identify your contribution to flourishing

This next area gets us beyond ourselves to think about how we can affect the world. As the civil rights leader Martin Luther King Jr. poignantly said, "Life's most persistent and urgent question is, 'What are you doing for others?'" Asking how we can leave the world better ensures we don't get stuck in a cycle of self-gratification but use our lives for something that matters.

The goal here is to help people and our planet flourish in the truest sense of the word. Flourishing is not the mere absence of conflict, but a deep sense of wholeness, justice, and peace—a concept captured in the Hebrew word *shalom*. How can you help people live together in greater harmony? Heal the environment to make the world better for our kids? Improve the quality of life for people who use your product? The scope of potential problems is broad, but the fundamental question here is: How can you give rather than merely take?

Which problems you decide to tackle will be informed by your values, life experience, and spiritual beliefs. Ask yourself, "How do I want to make a difference? What specific problems do I want to solve? Which injustices deserve my full devotion?" Think about this question not just in terms of the problems that present themselves to you now but also in terms of your legacy. When you're at the end of your life looking back, what kind of legacy do you want to have left behind? Why will the world be a better place because you were here?

This question can be daunting because of its scope. Our world certainly has no shortage of important problems that merit attention. Here, though, I agree with the humanitarian and U2 front man Bono: "I just hope when the day is done, I've been able to tear a little corner off of the darkness." Rather than being overwhelmed by the infinite problems in our world, Bono has chosen to use his platform to serve as a philanthropist and advocate for humanitarian issues. How will you go about making a difference? What can you do to "tear off a corner of the darkness" in your own sphere of influence?

Reflecting on these questions helped me realize that the problem I care most deeply about is ineffective leadership. Like most people, I've worked for enough bad bosses to realize how draining and limiting an ineffective leader can be—not just for the people underneath them, but for the whole organization. I've also seen so many friends stay stuck for too long because they didn't know which way was out. Both these situations break my heart because of the frustration and diminished impact they create.

Once you've worked for a great leader who frees you to do your best work, you never want to see anyone experience anything different. If you've ever brushed up against a leader with a clear and compelling purpose that gives them a laser focus, you also want that same sort of clarity yourself. Both these factors compel me to coach leaders toward the best versions of themselves—not just for their own benefit, but also for the sake of the people they influence.

As you also take time to connect your strengths and passions to a critical problem in the world, you'll find your purpose takes on an even deeper sense of meaning—a meaning that will be critical motivation as you embrace the sacrifices of humbler leadership.

Connect your purpose to your current reality

One of the natural byproducts of clarifying your purpose is the question, "What now?" Since clarity brings energy, a deeper understanding of your purpose will energize you to do something with it. This energy is great, but it's also frustrating for people who feel stuck in their jobs. If you want to join the Peace Corps but don't want to leave your partner and kids, what do you do?

Just as your eyes will be opened to new passions, strengths, and problems by examining the earlier questions, you can also find multiple opportunities to begin living out your purpose today if you take time to look. Ask yourself, "How could I use my strengths or passions today? How could I express this purpose in my current job? In my family? In my community?" Working toward a better future where you can embrace your purpose more fully does not preclude you from beginning to practice it now. In fact, I'd argue that practicing it today—even in circumstances that are not ideal—is a prerequisite for living it out in your next stage of life. As former Taylor University president Milo Rediger put it, "The faithfulness of today determines the task of tomorrow."

As I was preparing to leave my job in higher education, I was confronted by this gap between my purpose and my performance. I was spending my nights and weekends building workshops to help my clients grow in their leadership, yet the team I led in my day job was getting little of that same investment from me. I was struck by my hypocrisy. Who was I to advise leaders on how to coach and develop their people if I wasn't living it out myself? That realization fanned a new fire in me. I determined that as long as I remained in my current role, I wanted to be the world's best talent developer. If I was going to have any integrity in this new business, I had to practice what I preached by devoting significantly more time to training and coaching my people.

Although I fell far short of that "world's best" goal, I did begin making investments and seeing the consequent payoff. My staff grew, and I learned more about what worked and what didn't. I became acquainted with the struggles of holding people accountable, building ongoing development plans, and trying to train a staff with diverse skillsets and job responsibilities. Most importantly, I grew more into the kind of leader I was trying to create in my consulting practice. By finding ways to practice my purpose while still advancing the mission, vision, and values of my organization, I brought more energy to my work and helped move my team forward.

So how can you begin practicing your purpose within your day-to-day life? Does that mean volunteering in your community? Raising your hand for special projects at work? Or just becoming more intentional with how you approach the people and tasks you interact with every day? Answering this final question will humble you as you realize the bigger purposes your life was meant to advance and how you can begin living out your purpose today.

Humbler in Two Minutes

- **Reflect on your passions.** Ask yourself, "What's the best hour of my week, and why?"
- **Assess your strengths.** Ask a friend what strengths they see in you.
- **Identify your contribution to flourishing.** Make a list of problems in your community that you find yourself thinking about a lot.
- **Connect your purpose to your current reality.** Brainstorm a few ways you could start using your strengths or passions this week to contribute to greater flourishing.

Conclusion

In the late 1990s, a philanthropist in Lancaster, Pennsylvania found himself facing an unusual predicament: no one wanted his help. Or rather, they didn't want the kind of help he was offering.

After the fall of the Soviet Union in the 1990s, a businessperson named Jeff Rutt felt called to make a difference in the now-impoverished parts of Ukraine. With the support of his local church, Rutt led multiple mission trips to Eastern Europe, arms loaded with food, clothing, and medical supplies. For a man who'd spent years building homes in the U.S., the prospect of building something of even greater significance in the city of Zaporizhzhya was invigorating.

Until one day.

During a visit, a local clergyman pulled Rutt aside and gave him some feedback that was undoubtedly difficult to hear: he wasn't really helping. While his heart was in the right place, Rutt's charity was eroding the city's economy. Locals had become dependent on the church for handouts, cannibalizing the job market. And the Ukrainian entrepreneurs who were working hard to meet the demands of their city couldn't compete with the free goods now flooding the market. Charity was addressing the symptoms of the problem but was making the disease worse. His helping was hurting.

But rather than be insulted that his aid was not appreciated, Rutt went back to the drawing board—researching alternative means of alleviating poverty without sacrificing the dignity and

177

autonomy of the people he was trying to help. In that research process, he stumbled across microfinance, the process of giving entrepreneurs small loans they could use to invest in their own ideas to grow their own businesses.

In 1997, Rutt and his team gave out their first round of loans and were amazed to see the positive, sustainable results in the community. After years of trying and failing, his team had finally uncovered the strategy that would accomplish their true goal. It was then that HOPE International was born.

Few organizations I've come across better embody the ideals of humble leadership than HOPE. From its earliest days, HOPE's founders were animated by a **greater purpose** of alleviating spiritual and material poverty in underserved communities. That compelling purpose made them tenacious even in the face of setbacks. When told that their approach was wrong, they adopted a **growth mindset**, embracing the challenge rather than running away. But their humble leadership story doesn't stop there.

Several years later, the organization approached another decision point. Eager to expand its services to other communities that lacked reliable financial services, HOPE's **accurate self-perception** enabled them to recognize they could not scale their own organization quickly enough to meet all the needs presented to them. They needed partners—other organizations which already had the relationships and infrastructure needed to deliver these services in new countries. So rather than competing with these organizations for donors and staff, they started rooting for their rivals—giving their curriculum and business model away to others freely. By **appreciating others' contributions** and letting go of the need for credit, they catalyzed a much grander impact in the world.

HOPE International and its partners now serve 20 different countries around the world—a rapid pace of growth for an organization started just 25 years prior. By learning from the people they were serving, HOPE created a business model where 98% of its loans are repaid on time, with interest—a feat that makes their nonprofit remarkably sustainable. Humble leadership laid the foundation for the organization to get out of its own way, adapt its approach to accomplish the goal, and place the mission ahead of notoriety.

***

Imagine how different your organization would be if it adopted the humble approach to leadership that HOPE International embraced. Can you picture how much more successful your business would become if leaders truly began to listen to their customers and frontline employees? Can you visualize how much healthier your culture would be if managers placed the organization's grander purpose ahead of their own insecurities and turf battles? Humble leadership at this scale carries ripple effects that can change the world. And most importantly, this vision is within our capacity to create.

To be fair, that challenge is daunting. Transforming ourselves into humble leaders requires many slow, glamourless turns of the Do-Become Flywheel. We must set aside precious time to build a plan for our own development, and we must wisely consider which of the 10 mindsets and skillsets of humble leaders that we will prioritize. So for those of you who wonder if you have the courage needed for the journey ahead, I'll offer one final word of encouragement.

Perhaps it feels like becoming a humble leader just isn't in the cards for you. It seems like it's too late in life, or you're not wired for it, or your difficult boss just makes it impossible for you. And all that might be true. But imagine for a moment that you stopped thinking about where you're *not* and started asking yourself *Where am I going?* You stop asking "Am I a good leader?", "Am I a good parent?", "Am I a good friend?" and instead ask yourself a different question: *Am I stagnant, or am I growing?*

You ask that question, and then you make a choice. You choose the path of growth and the slow, almost imperceptible process of getting a little humbler every day. You embrace the mantra of "progress over perfection" and stop stressing about how far away the finish line appears to be.

And then one day, you wake up and notice things are a bit different. You're more patient, more kind, a better listener. The people around you are more energized as they see how their strengths enable them to produce fantastic results. That animosity you once had with a coworker has somehow morphed into a lighthearted friendship. The change is stark, but it didn't happen overnight. Looking back now, you realize the evolution was happening so slowly you didn't notice it. It's as if you were sitting on your back deck with a good friend late on a summer evening and suddenly realize it's dark.

Who knows? Maybe at your retirement party or your funeral, the people who knew you best would respect you the most. They'd say, "the most striking thing about them was their humility....it was never about them....they brought out the best in us." Maybe, just maybe, there's still time for you to rewrite your legacy.

I hope the insights you've found in the prior pages can help you better live out your vision and build a development plan that makes you more of the person you want to become. My greatest hope is that this book has made your journey toward humbler leadership more compelling and accessible. I honestly believe that your life and the lives of the people you touch will be greatly enriched as you become a humbler leader.

***

Want to keep growing? Check out the additional online resources by scanning the QR code here or visiting JoshWymore.com/humbler.

If You Enjoyed This...

If you loved this book, would you do two things for me?

1. **Text a friend about it.** All my favorite books have come via a recommendation from a friend, and you could be that friend to someone else.
2. **Take two minutes to write a review on Amazon.** This show of support raises the book's visibility and helps new folks find it as well.

While doing these two things would certainly help me, more importantly, they further shine a spotlight on humility. I think we can all agree that our world would be better if our friends, family, and coworkers were all a little humbler. Will you partner with me and help make humble leadership contagious?

Leave a review by using the QR code above or by searching Amazon for "humbler leadership."

Thanks for your support!

How to Become a Humbler Leader

If you want to enjoy all the personal and professional benefits of humility (happiness, stronger relationships, better performance, team engagement, and contagious humility), then you need a plan for your character development.

The best way to bridge the Transformation Gap is by practicing the four pillars of humble leadership. What you Do shapes who you Become, and vice versa.

Accurate Self-Perception

Increase your self-awareness [humility assessment, journaling], **embrace the Humility Paradox** [contemplate your gifts and shortcomings], and **practice metacognition** [state your assumptions, look "out the window" and "into the mirror."].

Appreciating Others' Strengths and Contributions

Ask open-ended questions ["How?" not "Could you?"], then **listen actively** [Why Am I Talking?]. **Invite others in** [the daily review, create a challenge network], and **solve problems with people, not for people** [frame the problem, not the solution]. Finally, **Become a Multiplier** [act like a talent scout, express appreciation for others].

Growth Mindset

Cultivate a growth mindset [progress over perfection, become a novice, let go of things you can't control].

Greater Purpose

Discern your purpose [passions + strengths + flourishing].

Acknowledgements

Writing this book was so humbling, as it gave me hundreds of chances to benefit from the contributions of others. While saying "thank you" here is far from adequate repayment, I'm grateful to have this chance to express my gratitude.

Many of these ideas first took root a decade ago thanks to role models and teachers who lived out these virtues. Brad Bowser, Stan Coppinger, and Scott Gaier: thanks for helping me fall in love with this virtue.

Several friends were generous enough to offer their feedback on a workshop based on this book. Jody Hirschy, Matt Konow, Arlan Friesen, Mario Baldassari, Kevin Butler, Jennifer Kasmier, Tony Opliger, Larry Rottmeyer, Ken Sipe, and Nick Dancer: thanks for your thoughtful insights!

I owe deep gratitude to the readers who patiently read the terrible early drafts of this manuscript and gave valuable feedback about what wasn't working. Nathan Heintzeman, Tim Herrmann, Mike Stone, Nathaniel Youndt, Kent Yost, Jan Yost, and Emily Wymore: this book would still be awful without your help.

I'm also grateful for the beta readers who helped refine the book as it prepared to cross the finish line. Nathan Heintzeman, Maria Lehr, Amos Norman, Chris Sloan, and Sally Stitzer: thank you for the hours you spent laboring alongside me as I worked to deliver this book.

Throughout this process, I've also benefited from the gracious assistance of professionals who've helped me locate critical research for the book (Elizabeth Walker and the rest of the Spring Arbor University library staff), navigate the path to publication (Sarah Westfall), edit this manuscript into something that was semi-logical (Sarah Chauncey) and clear (Idria Barone Knecht), and coach me along the way (Mike Anderson). Thank you all for your expert guidance and belief in this project.

I'm especially indebted to my inner circle for playing the roles of both challenger and supporter during this process. Emily Wymore, Nathan Heintzeman, and Kevin Butler walked with me weekly over the years that this book was coming into being. You loved me by asking the tough questions, and I'm so glad you did.

Thank you in particular, Emily, for helping me find the space to take on this audacious challenge and putting up with my nonstop talking about the book at all hours. The energy I've put into this book is nothing in comparison to the investment you've made into our family to keep our lives on track and on purpose over the last three years. I couldn't ask for a better partner and sounding board throughout this process. I love you.

Mom and Dad, thank you for being my biggest cheerleaders from Day 1. Your unwavering support has given me the confidence to do bold things.

Notes

Sir Isaac Newton said, "If I have seen further, it is by standing on the shoulders of giants." This was certainly true for me as I wrote *Humbler Leadership*. Writing this book prompted me to unlearn much of what I thought I knew about humility based on the incredible research that others have done. So to all the thought leaders and researchers who inspired this book, thank you. I'm deeply indebted.

Introduction

Nelson Mandela (pp. 1–3). The details of Mandela's story came from The Archive at the Centre of Memory. *Biography of Nelson Mandela.* https://www.nelsonmandela.org/content/page/biography

For more about the differences between restorative and retributive justice, see Allais, L. (2011). Restorative justice, retributive justice, and the South African Truth and Reconciliation Commission. *Philosophy & Public Affairs,* *39*(4), 331-363.

"while a native speaker may be the most natural *practitioner...*" (p. 5). Walkinshaw, I., & Oanh, D. H. (2014). Native and non-native English language teachers: Student perceptions in Vietnam and Japan. *SAGE Open,* *4*(2). https://doi.org/10.1177/2158244014534451

Chapter 1: Discovering Humility

"I was the Michael Scott of assistant softball coaches" (p. 11). Steve Carell's character in The Office provides a masterclass on what not to do in leadership.

Chapter 2: Defining Humble Leadership

Good to Great (pp. 16–19). The findings mentioned come directly from Collins, J. (2001). *Good to great: Why some Companies make the leap...and others don't*. Harper Collins.

Book sales numbers come from Harper Collins. https://www.harpercollins.com/products/good-to-great-jimcollins? variant= 32116997292066

Lee Iacocca (p. 18). Collins discusses Iacocca in *Good to Great*. Additional sources include McFadden, R. (2019, July 2). Lee Iacocca, visionary automaker who led both Ford and Chrysler, is dead at 94. *The New York Times*, 1–11. https://www.nytimes.com/2019/ 07/02/obituaries/lee-iacocca-dead.html

Surowiecki, J. (2002, July 22). Did Iacocca ruin American business? *The Guardian*, 1–10. https://www.theguardian.com/business/2002/jul/23/ enron.worldcom

Reuters Staff. (2019, July 2). 'I Am Chairman Of Chrysler Corporation Always': 8 facts about Lee Iacocca. *Reuters*. https://www.reuters.com/ article/us-people-lee-iacocca-facts/i-am-chairman-of-chrysler-corporation-always-8-facts-about-lee-iacocca-idUSKCN1TY06X

"the concept was not on the radar of the average leader" (p. 19). One measure of the public's fascination with humility in leadership is the number of business or psychology publications that feature the word "humility" in the title. From 1946–2000 (the year before *Good to Great* was published), *humility* appeared in 133 academic article or book titles. From 2001–2010 alone, that number leaps to 477. Even when accounting for the explosion in publishing that happened around that time, this jump is substantial. (See the graphic on p. 187.) It appears that our generation is rediscovering this ancient virtue.

"humility was seen as a symptom of low self-esteem" (p. 19). Weiss, H. M., & Knight, P. A. (1980). The utility of humility: Self-esteem, information search, and problem-solving efficiency. *Organizational Behavior and Human Performance*, 25: 216–223.

Definitions of humility (pp. 20–21). Definition #1 comes from Owens, B. P., & Hekman, D. R. (2012). Modeling how to grow: An inductive examination of humble leader behaviors, contingencies, and outcomes.

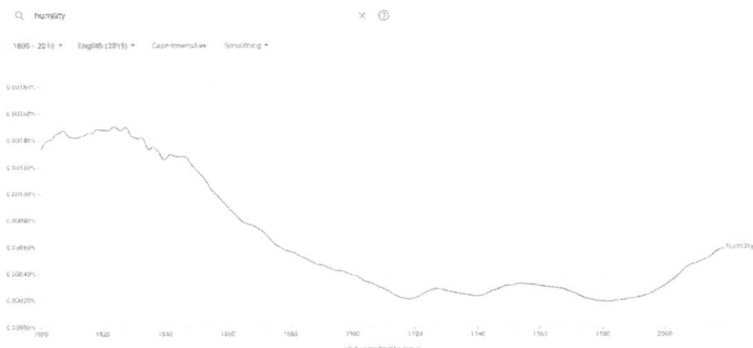

Academy of Management Journal, *55*(4), 787–818. https://doi.org/10.5465/amj.2010.0441.

Definition #2 comes from Gist, M. (2020). *The extraordinary power of leader humility*. Berret-Koehler.

Definition #3 comes from Davis, D. E., McElroy, S., Choe. E., Westbrook, C. J., DeBlaere, C., Van Tongeren, D. R., Hook, J., Sandage, S. J., & Placeres, V. (2017). Development of the experiences of humility scale. *Journal of Psychology and Theology*, *45*(1), 3–16. https://doi.org/10.1177/009164711704500101

Definition #4 comes from The Arbinger Institute. (2018). *Leadership and self-deception: Getting out of the box*. Berrett-Koehler. Although they don't explicitly label their "out of the box" thinking as humility, it's a terrific definition of it.

Definition #5 comes from Morris, J. A., Brotheridge, C. M., & Urbanski, J. C. (2005). Bringing humility to leadership: Antecedents and consequences of leader humility. *Human Relations*, *58*(10), 1323–1350. https://doi.org/10.1177/0018726705059929

Definition #6 comes from Department of the Army (2019, July 31). *Army leadership and the profession* (ADP 6-22). https://armypubs.army.mil/epubs/DR_pubs/DR_a/ARN20039-ADP_6-22-001-WEB-0.pdf

"humble literally means 'on the ground'…" (p. 22). Online Etymology Dictionary. (n.d.). Humble. https://www. etymonline.com/word/humble. **Mindset (pp. 22–23).** Dweck's book is certainly worth a read: Dweck, C. S. (2006). *Mindset. The new psychology of success*. Ballantine Books.

The Purpose-Driven Life (p. 24). Warren, R. (2002). *The purpose-driven life: What on Earth am I here for?* Zondervan.

"[Humble] leaders are incredibly ambitious…" (p. 25). Collins revisits these findings in Collins, J., & Lazier, B. (2020). *Beyond entrepreneurship 2.0: Turning your business into an enduring great company.* Portfolio

"Humbitious" (p. 25). The origin of this term is unclear, though earliest records suggest it originated at Bell Labs. For more, see Taylor, W. C. (2013). Are you humbitious enough to lead? *Daily Good.* http://www.dailygood.org/story/458/are-you-humbitious-enough-to-lead-william-c-taylor/

"Humility research captures this idea of a greater purpose…" (p. 25). "Transcendence" and "acceptance of something greater than the self" are terms used in Morris, J. A., Brotheridge, C. M., & Urbanski, J. C. (2005). Bringing humility to leadership: Antecedents and consequences of leader humility. *Human Relations, 58*(10), 1323–1350.

"Keeping one's place in the world in perspective" emerges from Tangney, J. P. (2000). Humility: Theoretical perspectives, empirical findings and directions for future research. *Journal of Social and Clinical Psychology, 19*(1), 70–82. https://doi.org/10.1521/jscp.2000.19.1.70

Satya Nadella (pp. 26–28). Microsoft's *Forbes* ranking comes from the 2021 *Fortune 500* rankings.

The industry expert prediction came from McCracken, H. (2017, September 18). *Satya Nadella rewrites Microsoft's code.* Fast Company. https://www.fastcompany.com/40457458/satya-nadella-rewrites-microsofts-code

The "hubris" and "if you just want to join a cool company" quotes come from an interview Nadella completed with Adam Grant at the Wharton School: Wharton University of Pennsylvania. (2018, February 27). *Authors at Warburton Satya Nadella* [Video]. YouTube. https://www.youtube.com/watch?v=gawGEyAS-rI

Microsoft's growth statistics ($300 billion and $2.5 trillion) come from Wadhwa, V., Amla, I., & Salkever, A. (2021, December 21). *How Microsoft made the stunning transformation from Evil Empire to Cool Kid.* Fortune. https://fortune.com/2021/12/21/microsoft-cultural-transformation-book-excerpt-satya-nadella/

Situational leadership and Transformational leadership (pp. 28–29). Yukl, G. (2013). *Leadership in organizations* (8th ed.). Pearson.

"great leadership requires 'more, but not less' than humility" (p. 29). Kevin delivered this gem on one of our Tuesday evening walks.

Chapter 3: The Personal Benefits of Humble Leadership

Humility quotes (p. 31). The Buddhism quote comes from the Study Buddhism. (n.d.). *Being humble.* https://studybuddhism.com/en/tibetan-buddhism/mind-training/commentaries-on-lojong-texts/commentary-on-eight-verses-of-mind-training-dr-berzin/being-humble

The Holy Bible, English Standard Version (2001). Bible Hub. https://biblehub.com/romans/12-3.htm

The Confucianism quote comes from Clare, I. S. (2009). *Library of universal history.* BiblioBazaar. (Original work published in 1908.)

The Islam quote comes from The Quran (T. Itani, Trans.). Clear Quran. https://www.clearquran.com/031.html

The Stoicism quote comes from Cicero. *De officiis.* (P. G. Wash, Trans.) Oxford University Press. (Original work published ca. 44 B.C.)

"In a national survey of 3,010 individuals…" (pp. 34–35). Krause, N., Pargament, K. I., Hill, P. C., & Ironson, G. (2016). Humility, stressful life events, and psychological well-being: Findings from the landmark spirituality and health survey. *Journal of Positive Psychology, 11*(5), 499–510. https://doi.org/10.1080/17439760.2015.1127991

"One meta-analysis of 72 studies…" (p. 35). Burnette, J. L., Knouse, L. E., Vavra, D. T., O'Boyle, E., & Brooks, M. A. (2020). Growth mindsets and psychological distress: A meta-analysis. *Clinical Psychology Review, Volume 77,* https://doi.org/10.1016/j.cpr.2020.101816.

"People would rather follow a leader who is always *real* rather than one who is always *right*" (p. 36). Groeschel, C. @craiggroeschel. *Be yourself. People would rather follow a leader who is always REAL than one who is always RIGHT.* Twitter, 2013, July 10. twitter.com/craiggroeschel/status/355012171115139072.

Pete Carroll (pp. 36–39). An engrossing overview of Carroll's history and the evolution of his philosophy can be found in Gulati, R., Breitfelder, M. D., & Burke, M. (2020). Pete Carroll: Building a winning organization through purpose, caring, and inclusion. *Harvard Business School Case N9-421–020*. Many of the quotes and much of the content in this section come from this case.

The "one of only three" stat comes from Getz, V. (2014, December 7). Head coaches that won both college titles and NFL Championships (or Super Bowls). Sports list of the day: Be in the know. *Sportsweek*. https://sportsweeksportslist.wordpress.com/2014/12/07/head-coaches-that-won-both-college-titles-and-nfl-championships-or-super-bowls/

The "It's not about winning on Sunday" quote and "always compete" philosophy is described Schottey, M. (2013). *Pete Carroll shares the Seahawks' winning philosophy with Bleacher Report*. Bleacher Report. https://bleacherreport.com/articles/1480332-pete-carroll-shares-the-seahawks-winning-philosophy-with-bleacher-report

The USC hall of fame is described Henson, S. (2021, November 28). *USC football coaches: Glory and gaffes, from Gloomy Gus to Lincoln Riley*. Los Angeles Times. https://www.latimes.com/sports/usc/story/ 2021-11-28/usc-football-coaches-list-john-mckay-gloomy-gus-john-robinson-pete-carroll-lincoln-riley

The "youngest team ever" stat was Pro Football Reference (2022, September 3). *Pete Carroll*. https://www.pro-football-reference.com/ coaches/CarrPe0.htm

"A survey of 1,500 people..." (p. 40). Goddard, H. W., Olson, J. R., Galovan, A. M., Schramm, D. G., & Marshall, J. P. (2016). Qualities of character that predict marital well-being. *Family Relations, 65*(3), 424–438. https://doi.org/10.1111/fare.12195

"Humble individuals are...more helpful, forgiving, generous, grateful, and cooperative" (p. 40). Nielsen, R., & Marrone, J. A. (2018). Humility: Our current understanding of the construct and its role in organizations. *International Journal of Management Reviews, 20*(4), 805–824. https://doi.org/10.1111/ijmr.12160

"humbler students outperformed their less humble peers" (pp. 42–43). Owens, B. P., Johnson, M. D., & Mitchell, T. R. (2013). Expressed humility in organizations: Implications for performance, teams, and leadership. *Organization Science, 24*(5), 1517–1538. https://doi.org/ 10.1287/orsc.1120.0795

"individuals who were both honest and humble..." (pp. 43–44). For more, see Science Daily. (2011, March 1). Higher job performance linked to people who are more honest and humble. *Science Daily.* https://www. sciencedaily.com/releases/ 2011/03/110301122059.htm

Promotion vs prevention focus (p. 44). Owens, B. P., & Hekman, D. R. (2016). How does leader humility influence team performance? Exploring the mechanisms of contagion and collective promotion focus. *Academy of Management Journal, 59*(3), 1088–1111. https://doi.org/10.5465/amj. 2013.0660

"college students who were paid to raise money by calling potential donors" (pp. 44–46). For more on Study #1, see Grant, A. M., Campbell, E. M., Chen, G., Cottone, K., Lapedis, D., & Lee, K. (2007). Impact and the art of motivation maintenance: The effects of contact with beneficiaries on persistence behavior. *Organizational Behavior and Human Decision Processes, 103*, 53–67. https://doi.org/ 10.1016/ j.obhdp.2006.05.004

For more on Study #2, Grant, A. M. (2008). The significance of task significance: Job performance effects, relational mechanisms, and boundary conditions. *The Journal of Applied Psychology, 93*(1), 108–124. https://doi.org/10.1037/0021-9010.93.1.108

Chapter 4: Humble Leadership's ROI

Kim Hayworth (pp. 47–50). Kim and I worked together from 2015-2019. I conducted these interviews in 2022.

"humble leaders generate more personal commitment to organizational goals" (p. 50). For more about the outcomes of humble leadership on followers, see Owens, B. P., Johnson, M. D., & Mitchell, T. R. (2013). Expressed humility in organizations: Implications for performance, teams, and leadership. *Organization Science, 24*(5), 1517–1538. https://doi.org/ 10.1287/orsc.1120.0795

...and Owens, B. P., & Hekman, D. R. (2016). How does leader humility influence team performance? Exploring the mechanisms of contagion and collective promotion focus. *Academy of Management Journal, 59*(3), 1088– 1111. https://doi.org/10.5465/amj.2013.0660

"team members are more resilient in the face of challenges..." (p. 50). This finding also comes from Owens, B. P., & Hekman, D. R. (2016). How does leader humility influence team performance? Exploring the mechanisms of contagion and collective promotion focus. *Academy of*

Management Journal, 59(3), 1088–1111. https://doi.org/10.5465/amj.2013.0660

"the average leader only engages about 34% of their people at any given point in time" (p. 50). Harter, J. (2018). *Employee engagement on the rise in the U.S.* Gallup. https://news.gallup.com/poll/ 241649/employee-engagement-rise.aspx

2% and 67% (pp. 50–51). These stats come from Gallup. (2014). *How to create a strengths-based organizational culture.* Gallup. https://www.gallup.com/cliftonstrengths/en/290903/how-to-create-strengths-based-company-culture.aspx

"Run the experiment" (p. 51). Rich shared this story at the Purpose Summit at The University of Notre Dame in 2022.

Cynt Marshall (pp. 52–56). Marshall's incredible story was synthesized from these sources:

Spears, M. J. (2022, May 9). *"We're not done yet": How Cynthia Marshall has helped transform the Mavericks.* Andscape. https://andscape.com/features/were-not-done-yet-how-cynthia-marshall-has-helped-transform-the-mavericks/

NBC 5 Dallas-Fort Worth. (2021, August 19). *Mavericks reportedly hire two time WNBA Champion Kristi Toliver as Assistant Coach.* https://www.nbcdfw.com/news/sports/mavericks-reportedly-hire-two-time-wnba-champion-kristi-toliver-as-assistant-coach/2722756/

Forbes. (2021, August 21). *How Dallas Mavericks CEO Cynt Marshall is shaping the NBA's future* [Video]. YouTube. https://www.youtube.com/watch?v=vHdNhUPv0-k

Jolee, T. (2021, February 10). *Lead with love: Mavs' artwork at Love Field aims to provide hope to travelers.* NBA. https://www.mavs.com/lovefield/

"In 2015, researchers Amy Ou, David Waldman, and Suzanne Peterson..." (p. 56). Firm performance in this study was measured as the net income of the past 12 months divided by the average total assets of those 12 months. This doesn't easily translate to a specific dollar value. Ou, A. Y., Waldman, D. A., & Peterson, S. J. (2018). Do humble CEOs matter? An examination of CEO humility and firm outcomes. *Journal of Management, 20(10)*, 1–27. https://doi.org/10.1177/0149206315604187

"balanced processing" (p. 56). Rego, A., Cunha, M. P. e., & Simpson, A. V. (2018). The perceived impact of leaders' humility on team effectiveness: An empirical study. *Journal of Business Ethics, 148*(1), 205–218. https://doi.org/10.1007/s10551-015-3008-3

"Happiness starts with a smile" (p. 57). Watch "Coca-Cola: Happiness starts with a smile" on YouTube. You can't help but smile.

"humble leadership itself is highly contagious" (pp. 57–58). Owens, B. P., & Hekman, D. R. (2012). Modeling how to grow: An inductive examination of humble leader behaviors, contingencies, and outcomes. *Academy of Management Journal, 55*(4), 787–818. https://doi.org/10.5465/amj.2010.0441

Ron Everly & Bill Jameson (pp. 58–59). These names are pseudonyms, but the college and its story are real. For more, see my dissertation: Wymore, J. A. (2016). College reimagined: A study of affordability & radical organizational change. [Doctoral dissertation, Pennsylvania State University] https://www.proquest.com/openview/025a4c5b99ba91d50dd 0241456811097/1?pq-origsite=gscholar&cbl=18750&diss=y

"Collins admitted, 'I still do not know the answer to that question'" (p. 61). Collins, J. (2001, January 1). Level 5 leadership: The triumph of humility and fierce resolve. *Harvard Business Review.* https://hbr.org/ 2001/01/level-5-leadership-the-triumph-of-humility-and-fierce-resolve-2

Chapter 5: The Do-Become Flywheel

What? So what? Now What? (p. 65). These questions seem to originate with Borton, T. (1970). *Reach, touch, and teach: Student concerns and process education.* McGraw-Hill.

Cathexis (p. 66). Merriam-Webster. (n.d.) Cathexis. In *Merriam-Webster.* https://www.merriam-webster.com/dictionary/cathexis

"a long obedience in the same direction" (p. 68). From Nietzsche as cited in Peterson, E. (1980). *A long obedience in the same direction.* Intervarsity Press.

"We are what we repeatedly do. Excellence, then, is not an act, but a habit" (p. 68) Huntress, C. (2017, August 24). *My favorite quote of all time is a misattribution.* Mission.org. https://medium.com/the-mission/my-favourite-quote-of-all-time-is-a-misattribution-66356f22843d

Atomic Habits (pp. 68–69). These quotes come from pages 36–39 of Clear, J. A. (2018). *Atomic habits: Tiny changes, remarkable results.* Penguin Random House.

Flywheels (p. 70). For more on the history and mechanics of flywheels, see Woodford, C. (2021). *Flywheels.* https://www.explainthatstuff.com/flywheels.html

"We are what we pretend to be" (p. 73). Vonnegut, K. (1962). *Mother night.* Random House Publishing Group.

"Would an idiot do that?" (p. 73). This quote comes from Forrester, B. (Writer) & Whedon, J. (Director). (2007, February 15). Business School (Season 3, Episode 17) [TV series episode] In Silverman, B. & Lieberstein, P. (Producers), *The Office.* NBC Universal Television Studio.

"cells that fire together, wire together" (p. 75). This quote comes from Shatz, C. J. (1992). The developing brain. *Scientific American, 267*(3), 60–67. http://www.jstor.org/stable/24939213. Although Shatz did not invent this concept (it's credited to psychologist Donald Hebb from 1949), she's the first to say it in this memorable fashion.

Chapter 6: Making a Plan for a Change

"If you fail to plan, you plan to fail" (p. 77). Quote Investigator. (2018, July 8). If you fail to prepare you are preparing to fail. *Quote Investigator.* https://quoteinvestigator.com/2018/07/08/plan/

Benjamin Franklin (pp. 77–79). All the Franklin quotes come from Franklin's autobiography, which can be found at Franklin, B. (1909). *The autobiography of Benjamin Franklin.* P. F. Collier & Son Company. (Original work published 1791). His spelling has been modernized.

The Road to Character (p. 79). Brooks, D. (2016). *The road to character.* Thorndike Press.

The 70:20:10 rule (pp. 80–81). McCall, M. W., Lombardo, M. M., & Morrison, A. M. (1988). *The lessons of experience: How successful executives develop on the job.* The Free Press.

"employees want more coaching from their managers…" (p. 82). DDI. (2019). *Frontline leader project.* https://www.ddiworld.com/research/frontline-leader-project

"most leaders actually use a 55:25:20 split" (p. 82). Global Leadership Forecast. (2011). *Ready-now leaders: 25 findings to meet tomorrow's business challenges.* DDI. https://media.ddiworld.com/ research/global-leadership-forecast-2014-2015_tr_ddi.pdf

"If you do commit to a clear goal, the goal-setting science shows you are more likely to take action and find success" (p. 84). Locke, E. A., & Latham, G. P. (2013). Goal setting theory: Theory building by induction. In Smith, K. G., & Hitt, M. A. (2005). *Great minds in management: The process of theory development.* Oxford University Press.

"11 times more likely" (p. 84). Norcross, J. C., Mrykalo, M. S., & Blagys, M. D. (2002). Auld lang syne: Success predictors, change processes, and self-reported outcomes of New Year's resolvers and nonresolvers. *Journal of Clinical Psychology, 58*(4), 397–405.

***Next Generation Leader* (p. 92).** Stanley, A. (2006). *Next generation leader: 5 essentials for those who will shape the future.* Multnomah.

Chapter 7: Increase Self-Awareness

"Individuals who lack self-awareness often have a hard time accepting feedback…" and **"while 95% of people think they're self-aware…" (p. 98).** For more, see Eurich, T. (2018, October 19). "Working with people who aren't self-aware." *Harvard Business Review.* https://hbr.org/2018/10/working-with-people-who-arent-self-aware

"many executives have disproportionately high evaluations of their own emotional intelligence" (p. 95). Sala, F. (2003). Executive blind spots: Discrepancies between self- and other-ratings. *Consulting Psychology Journal, 55*(4), 222–229. https://doi.org/10.1037/1061-4087.55.4.222

Johari window (p. 99). You can learn about the Johari window on Wikipedia, but for a more formal source, see Armstrong, T. R. (2006). Revisiting the Johari window: Improving communications through self-disclosure and feedback. *Human Development, 27*(2).

"we don't learn from experience; we learn from reflecting on experience" (p. 103). While this is commonly attributed to Dewey, there's no direct evidence he ever said it (though he said many things like it.) I can't find reliable evidence of who first said it.

"paying attention to the tension" (p. 105). This Andy Stanley-ism comes from Your Move with Andy Stanley. (2021). *How not to be your own worst enemy* *part 1: "Pay attention to the tension"* [Video]. YouTube. https://www.youtube .com/watch?v=6JRBeoVsWts

Chapter 8: Embrace the Humility Paradox

Humility paradox (pp. 106–110). Although this paradigm is my own creation, a similar version of this idea is the Daily Examen, a spiritual practice that was first conceived in 1522 by St. Ignatius of Loyola.

Chapter 9: Practice Metacognition

Cognitive biases (p. 112). For a quick overview of a number of cognitive biases, see Cherry, K. (2021, January 20). *List of common cognitive biases.* Verywellmind. https://www.verywellmind.com/ cognitive-biases-distort-thinking-2794763.

For more on the Fundamental Attribution Error, see Farnell, P., & Heberle, M. (2021, December 6). *The fundamental attribution error: Example, theory, & bias.* Study.com. https://study.com/learn/lesson/fundamental-attribution-error.html

For more on the recency bias (also called the availability heuristic), see Hayes, A. (2022, February 22). *Recency (availability) bias.* Investopedia. https://www.investopedia.com/recency-availability-bias-5206686

For more on the negativity bas, see The Decision Lab. (2022). *Why is the news always so depressing? The negativity bias, explained.* https:// thedecisionlab.com/biases/negativity-bias

Tripwires (p. 115). Heath, C., & Heath, D. (2013). *Decisive: How to make better choices in life and work.* Crown Business.

"The story I'm telling myself…" (p. 116). Brown, B. (2018). *Dare to lead.* Random House.

"almost unlimited ability to ignore our ignorance" (p. 118). Kahneman, D. (2011). *Thinking, fast and slow.* Farrar, Straus, and Giroux.

Restoration Therapy (pp. 118–120). Pfitzer, F., & Hargrave, T. (2011). *Restoration therapy: Understanding and guiding healing in marriage and family therapy.* Routledge.

Chapter 10: Ask Open-Ended Questions

"great listening is essential for great leadership" (p. 122). Research by DDI for instance finds that the #1 skill for leadership success is empathy. You simply can't empathize if you're not listening. For more see Sinar, E., Wellins, R., Paese, M., Smith, A., & Watt, B. (2016). *High-resolution leadership.* DDI. www.ddiworld.com/hirezleadership

Respectful inquiry (pp. 122–123). The control, competence, and connection terms are my own, but the concepts come from Van Quaquebeke, N., & Felps, W. (2018). Respectful inquiry: A motivational account of leading through asking questions and listening. *Academy of Management Review, 43*(1), 5–27. https://doi.org/10.5465/amr.2014.0537

"If your question has 'you' as the second word…" & "avoid 'Why' questions" (p. 124). I learned these concepts during my ICF coaching training with Creative Results Management.

Chapter 11: Listen Actively

"Leaders who refuse to listen will eventually be surrounded by people who have nothing significant to say" (p. 128). Stanley says this a lot. One such citation is here: @AndyStanley. "Leaders who refuse to listen will eventually be surrounded by people who have nothing significant to say." Twitter, 2011, August 17. https://twitter.com/andystanley/status/103841035108630528

"stay curious" (p. 129). Stanier, M.B. (2016). *The coaching habit: Say less, ask more & change the way you lead forever.* Page Two.

"Why Am I Talking?" (p 130). This acronym's origin is unclear. One such description is here: Bryant, A. (2019, January 9). *Before you speak, remember the W.A.I.T. acronym: "Why Am I Talking?"* PR Council. https://prcouncil.net/blog/speak-remember-w-t-acronym-talking/

Chapter 12: Invite Others In

"your college roommate" (p. 133). This research is summarized in Sacerdote, B. (2011). Peer effects in education: How might they work, how big are they and how much do we know thus far? *Handbook of the Economics of Education, 3*(11). https://doi.org/10.1016/B978-0-444-53429-3.00004-1

"Those peer effects continue after college" (pp. 133–134). The research on productivity comes from Falk, A., & Ichino, A. (2006). Clean evidence on peer effects. *Journal of Labor Economics, 24*(1), 39–57. https://doi.org/ 10.1086/497818

The research on perseverance comes from Buechel, B., Mechtenberg, L., Petersen, J. (2018). If I can do it, so can you! Peer effects on perseverance. *Journal of Economic Behavior & Organization,* 301–314. https://doi.org/ 10.1016/j.jebo.2018.09.004

The research on office lotteries comes from Lahno, A. M., & Serra-Garcia, M. (2015). Peer effects in risk taking: Envy or conformity? *Journal of Risk and Uncertainty, 50*(1), 73–95. https://doi.org/ 10.1007/s11166-015-9209-4

The research on a doctor's peer effects comes from Silver, D. (2021). Haste or waste? Peer pressure and productivity in the emergency department. *The Review of Economic Studies, 88*(3), 1385–1417. https://doi.org/10.1093/ restud/rdaa054

"you are the average of the five people you spend the most time with" **(p. 134).** This quote is commonly attributed to Jim Rohn, though I couldn't find the original source.

"Close relationships, more than money or fame, are what keep people happy…" (p. 134). Mineo, L. (2017, April 11). *Good genes are nice, but joy is better.* The Harvard Gazette. https://news.harvard.edu/ gazette/story/2017/04/over-nearly-80-years-harvard-study-has-been-showing-how-to-live-a-healthy-and-happy-life/

"People are *not* your most important asset. The *right* people are" (p. 135). Collins, J. (2001). *Good to great: Why some Companies make the leap...and others don't.* Harper Collins., p. 13

Support and challenge networks (p. 136). Grant, A. (2021). *Think again: The power of knowing what you don't know.* Viking.

Pixar (p. 137). Iwerks, P. (Director, Writer, Producer). (2007). *The Pixar story* [Film]. Leslie Iwerks Productions; Pixar Animation Studios.

The statistics on Pixar's success come from Bean, T. (2020, March 15). *Box office: 'Onward' & coronavirus hand Pixar its worst 10-day start ever.* Forbes. https://www.forbes.com/sites/travisbean/2020/03/15/box-office-onward--coronavirus-hand-pixar-worst-10-day-start-ever/

…and Brown, T. (2021, April 25). *'Soul' gives Pixar its 11th feature Oscar. Here's why Kemp Powers was not a nominee.* Los Angeles Times.

https://www.latimes.com/entertainment-arts/movies/story/2021-04-25/oscars-2021-soul-pixar-animated-winner-kemp-powers

"We don't rise to the level of our goals; we fall the level of our systems" (p. 139). Clear, J. @JamesClear. "You do not rise to the level of your goals. You fall to the level of your systems." Twitter, 2018, October 3. twitter.com/jamesclear/status/1047643455722283009.

Chapter 13: Solve Problems with People, Not for People

"women tend to undervalue their own abilities" (p. 145). Kuhn, P. J., & Villeval, M. C. (2013). *Are women more attracted to cooperation than men?* (Working Paper No. 52). National Bureau of Economic Research. https://www.nber.org/ papers/w19277

Additionally, see Woolley, A. W., Chabris, C. F., Pentland, A., Hashmi, N., & Malone, T. W. (2010). Evidence for a collective intelligence factor in the performance of human groups. *Science, 330*(6004), 686–688. https://doi.org/10.1126/science.1193147

"Seek first to understand, then to be understood" (p. 167). This quote is from the sage Stephen R. Covey in Covey, S. T. (2013, November 21). *The 7 habits of highly effective people.* Simon & Schuster.

Chapter 14: Become a Multiplier

"Anita Williams Woolley and her colleagues decided to test a few fascinating hypotheses about group intelligence" (pp. 148–149). Woolley, A. W., Chabris, C. F., Pentland, A., Hashmi, N., & Malone, T. W. (2010). Evidence for a collective intelligence factor in the performance of human groups. *Science, 330*(6004), 686–688. https://doi.org/10.1126/science.1193147

"words create worlds" (p. 152). Heschel, J. A. (1997). *Moral grandeur and spiritual audacity: Essays.* Farrar, Straus and Giroux.

Michelle Obama (p. 152). Obama, M. (2019). *Becoming.* Crown.

"never stifle a generous impulse" (p. 152). Jim Collins cites Packard in his book Collins, J., & Lazier, W. (2020). *Beyond entrepreneurship 2.0: Turning your business into an enduring great company.* Portfolio

"unexpressed gratitude is experienced as ingratitude" (p. 152). Andy Stanley. (2021). *Give thanks: An attitude of gratitude // Andy Stanley* [Video]. YouTube. https://www.youtube.com/watch?v= U7aneTHx2iw

Chapter 15: Cultivate a Growth Mindset

"leaders with a growth mindset share two elements: the right goal, and the right attribution" (p. 156). Yeager, D. S., & Dweck, C. S. (2020). What can be learned from growth mindset controversies? *American Psychologist, 75*(9), 1269–1284. https://doi.org/ 10.1037/amp0000794. supp

"The best way to *prove* yourself is to show that you're willing to *improve* yourself" (p. 159). Grant, A. *How to love criticism* [Video]. TED Conferences. https://www.ted.com/talks/worklife_with_adam_grant_ how_to_love_criticism/transcript?referrer=playlist-worklife_with _adam_grant

"Feedsmacked" (p. 163). Grenny, J. (2019). How to be resilient in the face of harsh criticism. *Harvard Business Review.* https://hbr.org/2019/ 06/how-to-be-resilient-in-the-face-of-harsh-criticism

"what got you here won't get you there" (p. 165). Goldsmith, M., & Reiter, M. (2007) *What got you here won't get you there: How success people become even more successful.* Hyperion.

Chapter 16: Discern Your Purpose

"He who has a 'why' to live can bear almost any 'how'." (p. 168). This quote comes from Nietzsche, F. (1997). *Twilight of the idol* (R. Polt, Trans.). Hackett Publishing Company Inc. (Original work published in 1889).

Florence Nightingale (pp. 169–170). Overall details of Nightingale's life come from History.com Editors. (2022, March 9). *Florence Nightingale.* History. https://www.history.com/topics/womens-history/florence-nightingale-1

…and Young, P., Hortis De Smith, V., Chambi, M. C., & Finn, B. C. (2011). Florence Nightingale (1820–1910), 101 years after her death. *Revista medica de Chile, 139*(6), 807–813. https://pubmed. ncbi.nlm.nih.gov/22051764/

Details about Westminster Abbey came from Pathmanathan, S. (n.d.). *Who's buried in Westminster Abbey?* The London Pass. https://londonpass.com/en-us/blog/whos-buried-in-westminster-abbey

"three elements of purpose" (p. 170). A similar idea is the concept of *ikigai.* For more on that concept, see Gaines, J. (2020, November 17). *The philosophy of ikigai: 3 examples about finding purpose.* PositivePsychology.com https://positivepsychology.com/ikigai/

"Life's most persistent and urgent question is, 'What are you doing for others?'" (p. 173). Read more about the context of this quote at PDE Press and Communications Office. (2020, January 2016). *A day on, not off.*

Shalom (p. 173). This is my paraphrase of Cornelius Plantinga Jr.'s definition found at Plantinga Jr., C. (1996, February 6). *Not the way it's supposed to be: A breviary of sin.* Eerdmans.

"I just hope when the day is done I've been able to tear a little corner off of the darkness" (p. 174). The quote origin is unclear, but it's consistently attributed to Bono. For more, see Lowe, L. (2018, May 10). *13 inspiring quotes from Bono on faith, music and social justice.* Parade Entertainment. https://parade.com/669054/lindsaylowe/13-inspiring-quotes-from-bono-on-faith-music-and-social-justice/

"The faithfulness of today determines the task of tomorrow" (p. 175). This quote was verbally conveyed to me in 2008 by one of Rediger's mentees, former Taylor president Jay Kesler.

Chapter 17: Conclusion

Hope International (pp. 177–179). Overall details about Hope came from Hope International. (2022). *How HOPE began.* https://www.hopeinternational.org/about-us/history/

You can read more about their rooting for rivals philosophy in their book of the same name. Greer, P., & Horst, C. (2018). *Rooting for rivals: How collaboration and generosity increase the impact of leaders, charities, and churches.* Bethany House Publishers.

Additional details about Hope came from Board of Directors. (2021). *HOPE International: Consolidated financial statements and report of independent certified public accountants.* HOPE International. https://www.hopeinternational.org/about-us/financials

...and the Hope International 2020 annual report, also found at https://www.hopeinternational.org/about-us/financials

Index

Note: Page numbers in *italics* indicate figures.

Index

About the Author

Dr. Josh Wymore has a passion for helping people live and lead with purpose and clarity. As an executive coach, consultant, and trainer with WYMORE, Josh has helped nonprofit and Fortune 500 leaders all around the world lead themselves and their teams more purposefully. He loves helping people leverage their strengths, develop a growth mindset, and become humbler leaders.

Josh grew up on a Christian campground in the Texas countryside where the most common forms of entertainment were playing six-man football and chasing armadillos. Before becoming a management consultant, Josh spent a decade in higher education developing leaders as an administrator and adjunct professor. Along the way, he obtained his PhD from The Pennsylvania State University. He and his family now proudly call Fort Wayne, IN, home.

***

Want to bring humbler leadership to your team or organization? Visit JoshWymore.com to learn more about keynotes, trainings, and coaching. You can also learn more about bulk book purchases for team development by contacting Josh at JoshWymore.com.

Lightning Source UK Ltd.
Milton Keynes UK
UKHW040951250123
415939UK00004B/273

9 798987 102510